S

R 66306.

THE NEW TEMPLE SHAKESPEARE

Edited by M. R. Ridley, M.A.

JULIUS CÆSAR

by William Shakespeare

London: J. M. DENT & SONS LTD.
New York: E. P. DUTTON & CO. INC.

BOOK
PRODUCTION
WAR ECONOMY
STANDARD

Editor's General Note

The Text. The editor has kept before him the aim of presenting to the modern reader the nearest possible approximation to what Shakespeare actually wrote. The text is therefore conservative, and is based on the earliest reliable printed text. But to avoid distraction (*a*) the spelling is modernised, and (*b*) a limited number of universally accepted emendations is admitted without comment. Where a Quarto text exists as well as the First Folio the passages which occur only in the Quarto are enclosed in square brackets [ ] and those which occur only in the Folio in brace brackets { }.

Scene Division. The rapid continuity of the Elizabethan curtainless production is lost by the 'traditional' scene divisions. Where there is an essential difference of place these scene divisions are retained. Where on the other hand the change of place is insignificant the scene division is indicated only by a space on the page. For ease of reference, however, the 'traditional' division is retained at the head of the page and in line numbering.

Notes. Passages on which there are notes are indicated by a † in the margin.

Punctuation adheres more closely than has been usual to the 'Elizabethan' punctuation of the early texts. It is often therefore more indicative of the way in which the lines were to be delivered than of their syntactical construction.

Glossaries are arranged on a somewhat novel principle, not alphabetically, but in the order in which the words or phrases occur. The editor is much indebted to Mr J. N. Bryson for his collaboration in the preparation of the glossaries.

Preface

The Text. The play was printed for the first time in the First Folio. It is exceptionally accurate; apart from a few instances of confusion in proper names and a certain amount of transposed punctuation, there are very few obvious errors; and the punctuation is both careful and interesting. Attention is drawn on the notes to a few passages which illustrate the methods of Elizabethan punctuation, and the effects produced by it.

Date of Composition. This can be determined with reasonable certainty within narrow limits. Meres does not mention it in 1598 (though that is no more than negative evidence); Weever, in his *Mirror of Martyrs*, which was published in 1601, but on the testimony of its author was 'fit for the print' two years earlier, alludes to the funeral speeches of Brutus and Antony; there is an almost certain reference to III. ii. 107 in Jonson's *Every Man Out of his Humour* (1599), III. iv. 33, and a more dubious reference in the same play to 'Et tu, Brute'; and one Thomas Platter saw a Cæsar play (which was probably ours) in September 1599 in London. Since metrical tests agree, we shall not be far out in attributing the play to 1598-99.

Source. Shakespeare's chief source is, as for his other Roman plays, North's translation of *Plutarch's Lives*, in this case the lives of Brutus, Cæsar, and Antony. The indebtedness is continuous and can be observed even in small details, such as the illness of Ligarius, and the manner of Portia's death; and it is therefore the more noteworthy that there is no suggestion in North of the actual language of the two great speeches of Brutus and Antony.

Duration of Action.　For purposes of his drama Shakespeare has rigorously compressed historical time. In fact Cæsar's triumph over the Pompeians was in October of 45 B.C.; he refused the crown at the Lupercalia on the 15th of February of 44 B.C., and was killed on the 15th of March; four or five days elapsed between his death and his funeral, and Octavius did not reach Rome till May. The events of this seven months Shakespeare compresses into a crowded period of thirty-six hours or so,[1] during which the action is practically continuous. After the end of Act III we can assume what interval we like, though if, as is most natural, we take the meeting in IV. i. to be that arranged for at the end of III. ii., the interval must be very short, whereas it was in fact eighteen months. About a year intervenes between the first and second scenes of Act IV, and between Act IV and Act V enough time for the transference of the army from Sardis to Philippi, though, in fact, and unless our geographical sense is acutely awake, we are not aware of any considerable gap. In the last Act the gap of twenty days between the two battles of Philippi is not indicated at all. From the dramatic point of view the play in fact falls into three main blocks of time, in each of which the action is continuous, and the extent of time-interval between which is unimportant. (Acts I.-III., Act IV. ii. and iii., and Act V., with a brief interlude, IV. i., which serves to link the two main sections of the play.)

---

[1] It is usual to assume an interval after I. ii., mainly on the grounds that Cassius' first 'whetting' of Brutus (II. i. 61) must be the conversation of I. ii. But I think it will be found on an examination of details that this interval creates as much trouble as it solves.

Criticism. Critics have vexed themselves, I think unnecessarily, in the attempt to determine ' who is the hero of *Julius Cæsar*.' It is true that if, paying too much attention to the fact that the play is called a tragedy, we therefore expect to find it adhering to the norm of the four great tragedies, we find ourselves at once in difficulties. We expect in the first place to find that Cæsar, who gives his name to the play, and is the most important figure in it, at least historically, is the hero; but he disappears from the stage halfway through the play, and even while he is on it we cannot feel him to be in the least ' interesting ' as the other tragic heroes are interesting. Nor do attempts to meet this difficulty by regarding the hero of the play as something so intangible as ' the spirit of Cæsar ' or ' Cæsarism ' carry any conviction, Shakespeare being a dramatist and not a political pamphleteer. Brutus, on the other hand, is a far more interesting figure, but apart from the fact that the internal conflict, which we watch with such strained attention in Hamlet and Macbeth, is in Brutus all but over before the play begins, most readers also feel that in some way Brutus never rises to the ' stature ' of the great tragic heroes. The truth surely is that the play is an extremely interesting transitional play or bridge between the chronicles and the tragedies. If it were a chronicle play, as one imagines it started out to be, then beyond question Cæsar would have been the full hero; if it had been designed from the outset as a tragedy, of the type of *Hamlet* or *Macbeth*, then equally beyond question Brutus would have been the hero, since he alone of the characters shows that capacity for internal conflict which Shakespeare felt to be of such tragic import. But since the play is part chronicle and part tragedy (in the Shakespearean sense) the heroship has been, as it were, put in commission, and the qualities and dramatic functions which in the later plays are concentrated in one figure are here shared between at least two, with perhaps some residue to be found in both Cassius and Antony. That may or may not be a good way to write a play, but it is idle to quarrel with Shakespeare and distract ourselves from the just appreciation of the play as it stands, because he did not, at this stage of his dramatic career, conform to a type of drama towards which he was feeling his way.

There is another odd feature about this play which is worth a passing mention; that is the discrepancy, most unusual in Shakespeare, between what is said about the two main figures by other characters, and the impression which they themselves produce upon us. Cæsar, as others speak of him, is the great conqueror and ruler of the world. Cassius, however bitterly he may resent the fact that he bestrides the petty world like a Colossus, none the less admits the fact; to Antony he is the noblest man that ever lived in the tide of times. But when Shakespeare presents him he not only goes out of his way to stress his physical infirmities, but also puts into his mouth phrase after phrase of the worst kind of egotistical rant, about the northern star, and two lions littered in one day, and so on. Is this perhaps merely that one of the things which at no period of his dramatic career could Shakespeare compass was the inspired rant of Marlowe; that he meant Cæsar to speak in the tones of the great ruler, and made him speak like a Byronic poseur? And again, more could hardly be said of any man than is said of Brutus by the conspirators at the beginning of the play and in Antony's superb tribute at the end; whereas most readers find in the Brutus which Shakespeare presents so complete a lack of practical wisdom, together with a good deal of the doctrinaire and a little of the prig, that not all the essential nobility of his idealism can make them ready to accept these encomia as just.

Johnson.— Of this tragedy many particular passages deserve regard, and the contention and reconcilement of Brutus and Cassius is universally celebrated, but I have never been strongly agitated in perusing it, and think it somewhat cold and unaffecting compared with some other of Shakespeare's plays; his adherence to the real story and to Roman manners seem to have impeded the natural vigour of his genius.

Hazlitt.—Shakespear's *Julius Cæsar* is not equal, as a whole, to either of his other plays taken from the Roman history. It is inferior in interest to *Coriolanus*, and both in interest and power to *Antony and Cleopatra*. It however abounds in admirable and affecting passages, and is remarkable for the profound knowledge of character, in which Shakespeare could scarcely fail. If there is any exception to this remark, it is in the hero of the piece himself. We do not much admire the representation here given of Julius Cæsar, nor do we think it answers to the portrait given of him in his Commentaries. He makes several vapouring and rather pedantic speeches, and does nothing. . . . The whole design to liberate their country fails from the generous temper and over-weening confidence of Brutus in the goodness of their cause and the assistance of others. . . . Cassius was better cut out for a conspirator. His heart prompted his head. His habitual jealousy made him fear the worst that might happen, and his irritability of temper added to his inveteracy of purpose, and sharpened his patriotism. The mixed nature of his motives made him fitter to contend with bad men.

Bradley.—If we consider the tragedies first on the side of their substance, we find at once an obvious difference between the first two and the remainder. Both Brutus and Hamlet are highly intellectual by nature and reflective by habit. Both may even be called, in a popular sense, philosophic; Brutus may be called so in a stricter sense. Each, being also a 'good' man, shows accordingly, when placed in critical circumstances, a sensitive and almost painful anxiety to do right. And though they fail—of course in quite different ways—to deal successfully with these circumstances, the failure in each case is connected rather with their intellectual nature and reflective habit than with any yielding to passion. Hence the name "tragedy of thought," which Schlegel gave to *Hamlet*, may be given also, as in effect it has been by Professor Dowden, to *Julius Cæsar*.

THE TRAGEDY OF JULIUS CÆSAR

DRAMATIS PERSONÆ

JULIUS CÆSAR.
OCTAVIUS CÆSAR, ⎫
MARCUS ANTONIUS, ⎬ *triumvirs after the death of Julius Cæsar.*
M. ÆMIL. LEPIDUS, ⎭
CICERO, ⎫
PUBLIUS, ⎬ *senators.*
POPILIUS LENA, ⎭
MARCUS BRUTUS, ⎫
CASSIUS, ⎪
CASCA ⎪
TREBONIUS, ⎪
LIGARIUS, ⎬ *conspirators against Julius Cæsar.*
DECIUS BRUTUS, ⎪
METELLUS CIMBER, ⎪
CINNA, ⎭
FLAVIUS and MARULLUS, *tribunes.*
ARTEMIDORUS of Cnidos, *a teacher of Rhetoric.*
A Soothsayer.
CINNA, *a poet.*   Another Poet.
LUCILIUS, ⎫
TITINIUS, ⎪
MESSALA, ⎬ *friends to Brutus and Cassius.*
Young CATO, ⎪
VOLUMNIUS, ⎭
VARRO, ⎫
CLITUS, ⎪
CLAUDIUS, ⎬ *servants to Brutus.*
STRATO, ⎪
LUCIUS, ⎭
DARDANIUS.
PINDARUS, *servant to Cassius.*

CALPURNIA, *wife to Cæsar.*
PORTIA, *wife to Brutus.*

Senators, Citizens, Guards, Attendants, &c.

SCENE: *Rome ; the neighbourhood of Sardis ; the neighbourhood of Philippi.*

THE TRAGEDY OF JULIUS CÆSAR

Act First

SCENES I, II, AND III

Rome.   A street

Enter Flavius, Marullus, and certain Commoners

Fla. Hence ! home, you idle creatures, get you home :
    Is this a holiday ? what, know you not
    (Being mechanical) you ought not walk
    Upon a labouring day, without the sign
    Of your profession ?   Speak, what trade art thou ?

1.C. Why, sir, a carpenter.

Mar. Where is thy leather apron, and thy rule ?
    What dost thou with thy best apparel on ?
    You, sir, what trade are you ?

2.C. Truly, sir, in respect of a fine workman,   10
    I am but, as you would say, a cobbler.

Mar. But what trade art thou ? answer me directly.

2.C. A trade, sir, that I hope I may use with a safe con-
science, which is indeed, sir, a mender of bad soles.

Fla. What trade, thou knave ? thou naughty knave, what
       trade ?

2.C. Nay, I beseech you, sir, be not out with me : yet if
    you be out, sir, I can mend you.

Mar. What mean'st thou by that ? mend me, thou saucy
    fellow ?

2.C. Why, sir, cobble you.   20

Fla. Thou art a cobbler, art thou ?

2.C. Truly, sir, all that I live by is with the awl : I meddle
    with no tradesman's matters, nor women's matters ;
    but withal I am indeed, sir, a surgeon to old shoes ; †
    when they are in great danger, I recover them. As
    proper men as ever trod upon neats-leather have
    gone upon my handiwork.

Fla. But wherefore art not in thy shop to-day ?
    Why dost thou lead these men about the streets ?

2.C. Truly, sir, to wear out their shoes, to get myself into   30
    more work. But indeed, sir, we make holiday to see
    Cæsar, and to rejoice in his triumph.

Mar. Wherefore rejoice ? What conquest brings he home ?
    What tributaries follow him to Rome,
    To grace in captive bonds his chariot-wheels ?
    You blocks, you stones, you worse than senseless
        things !
    O you hard hearts, you cruel men of Rome,
    Knew you not Pompey ? Many a time and oft
    Have you climb'd up to walls and battlements,

To towers and windows, yea, to chimney-tops, 40
Your infants in your arms, and there have sat
The live-long day, with patient expectation,
To see great Pompey pass the streets of Rome :
And when you saw his chariot but appear,
Have you not made an universal shout,
That Tiber trembled underneath her banks
To hear the replication of your sounds,
Made in her concave shores ?
And do you now put on your best attire ?
And do you now cull out a holiday ? 50
And do you now strew flowers in his way,
That comes in triumph over Pompey's blood ?
Be gone,
Run to your houses, fall upon your knees,
Pray to the gods to intermit the plague
That needs must light on this ingratitude.

Fla. Go, go, good countrymen, and, for this fault,
Assemble all the poor men of your sort ;
Draw them to Tiber banks, and weep your tears
Into the channel, till the lowest stream 60
Do kiss the most exalted shores of all.

Exeunt all the Commoners

See, whe'er their basest metal be not mov'd ;
They vanish tongue-tied in their guiltiness.

Go you down that way towards the Capitol,
This way will I : disrobe the images,
If you do find them deck'd with ceremonies.

Mar. May we do so ?
You know it is the feast of Lupercal.

Fla. It is no matter, let no images
Be hung with Cæsar's trophies : I 'll about,   70
And drive away the vulgar from the streets ;
So do you too, where you perceive them thick.
These growing feathers, pluck'd from Cæsar's wing,
Will make him fly an ordinary pitch,
Who else would soar above the view of men,
And keep us all in servile fearfulness.   *Exeunt*

*Flourish. Enter Cæsar; Antony, for the course; Calpurnia,
Portia, Decius, Cicero, Brutus, Cassius, Casca, and
Soothsayer : after them Marullus and Flavius*

Cæs. Calpurnia !

Csc.   Peace, ho ! Cæsar speaks.

Cæs.   Calpurnia !

Cal. Here, my lord.

Cæs. Stand you directly in Antonius' way,
　　When he doth run his course.　　Antonius !
Ant. Cæsar, my lord ?
Cæs. Forget not in your speed, Antonius,
　　To touch Calpurnia ; for our elders say,
　　The barren, touched in this holy chase,
　　Shake off their sterile curse.
Ant. 　　　　　　　　　　I shall remember :
　　When Cæsar says ' do this,' it is perform'd.　　　　10
Cæs. Set on, and leave no ceremony out.　　　*Flourish*
Soo. Cæsar !
Cæs. Ha ! who calls ?
Csc. Bid every noise be still : peace yet again !
Cæs. Who is it in the press that calls on me ?
　　I hear a tongue shriller than all the music
　　Cry ' Cæsar.'　Speak ; Cæsar is turn'd to hear.
Soo. Beware the Ides of March.
Cæs. 　　　　　　　　　　What man is that ?
Bru. A soothsayer bids you beware the Ides of March.
Cæs. Set him before me, let me see his face.　　　　20
Cas. Fellow, come from the throng, look upon Cæsar.
Cæs. What say'st thou to me now ? speak once again.
Soo. Beware the Ides of March.
Cæs. He is a dreamer, let us leave him : pass.
　　　　　　Sennet.　Exeunt all but Brutus and Cassius

5

Cas. Will you go see the order of the course ?

Bru. Not I.

Cas. I pray you do.

Bru. I am not gamesome : I do lack some part
Of that quick spirit that is in Antony.
Let me not hinder, Cassius, your desires ;   30
I 'll leave you.

Cas. Brutus, I do observe you now of late :
I have not from your eyes that gentleness
And show of love, as I was wont to have :
You bear too stubborn and too strange a hand
Over your friend, that loves you.

Bru.   Cassius,
Be not deceiv'd : if I have veil'd my look,
I turn the trouble of my countenance
Merely upon myself.   Vexed I am
Of late, with passions of some difference,   40
Conceptions only proper to myself,
Which give some soil perhaps to my behaviours ;
But let not therefore my good friends be griev'd
(Among which number, Cassius, be you one)
Nor construe any further my neglect,
Than that poor Brutus, with himself at war,
Forgets the shows of love to other men.

Cas. Then, Brutus, I have much mistook your passion,

By means whereof, this breast of mine hath buried
Thoughts of great value, worthy cogitations.   50
Tell me, good Brutus, can you see your face ?

Bru. No, Cassius ; for the eye sees not itself
But by reflection, by some other things.

Cas. 'Tis just,
And it is very much lamented, Brutus,
That you have no such mirrors, as will turn
Your hidden worthiness into your eye,
That you might see your shadow.   I have heard,
Where many of the best respect in Rome
(Except immortal Cæsar) speaking of Brutus,   60
And groaning underneath this age's yoke,
Have wish'd, that noble Brutus had his eyes.

Bru. Into what dangers would you lead me, Cassius,
That you would have me seek into myself,
For that which is not in me ?

Cas. Therefore, good Brutus, be prepar'd to hear :
And since you know you cannot see yourself
So well as by reflection, I your glass
Will modestly discover to yourself
That of yourself which you yet know not of.   70
And be not jealous on me, gentle Brutus :
Were I a common laugher, or did use
To stale with ordinary oaths my love

7

To every new protester ; if you know
That I do fawn on men, and hug them hard,
And after scandal them ; or if you know
That I profess myself in banqueting
To all the rout, then hold me dangerous

Flourish and shout

Bru. What means this shouting ? I do fear, the people
Choose Cæsar for their king.

Cas.   Ay, do you fear it ?   80
Then must I think you would not have it so.

Bru. I would not, Cassius, yet I love him well :
But wherefore do you hold me here so long ?
What is it, that you would impart to me ?
If it be aught toward the general good,
Set honour in one eye, and death i' the other,
And I will look on both indifferently :
For let the gods so speed me, as I love
The name of honour more than I fear death.

Cas. I know that virtue to be in you, Brutus,   90
As well as I do know your outward favour.
Well, honour is the subject of my story :
I cannot tell what you and other men
Think of this life : but, for my single self,
I had as lief not be, as live to be
In awe of such a thing as I myself.

I was born free as Cæsar, so were you,
We both have fed as well, and we can both
Endure the winter's cold as well as he :
For once, upon a raw and gusty day,   100
The troubled Tiber chafing with her shores,
Cæsar said to me ' Dar'st thou, Cassius, now
Leap in with me into this angry flood,
And swim to yonder point ? '   Upon the word,
Accoutred as I was, I plunged in,
And bade him follow : so indeed he did.
The torrent roar'd, and we did buffet it
With lusty sinews, throwing it aside,
And stemming it with hearts of controversy ;
But ere we could arrive the point propos'd,   110
Cæsar cried, ' Help me, Cassius, or I sink ! '
I (as Æneas, our great ancestor,
Did from the flames of Troy upon his shoulder
The old Anchises bear) so, from the waves of Tiber
Did I the tired Cæsar : and this man
Is now become a god, and Cassius is
A wretched creature, and must bend his body,
If Cæsar carelessly but nod on him.
He had a fever when he was in Spain,
And when the fit was on him, I did mark   120
How he did shake : 'tis true, this god did shake,

His coward lips did from their colour fly,
And that same eye, whose bend doth awe the world,
Did lose his lustre : I did hear him groan :
Ay, and that tongue of his, that bade the Romans
Mark him, and write his speeches in their books,
Alas, it cried, ' Give me some drink, Titinius,'
As a sick girl.   Ye gods, it doth amaze me,
A man of such a feeble temper should
So get the start of the majestic world,   130
And bear the palm alone.   *Shout.   Flourish*

Bru. Another general shout ?
I do believe that these applauses are
For some new honours, that are heap'd on Cæsar.

Cas. Why, man, he doth bestride the narrow world
Like a Colossus, and we petty men
Walk under his huge legs, and peep about
To find ourselves dishonourable graves.
Men at some time are masters of their fates :
The fault (dear Brutus) is not in our stars,   140
But in ourselves, that we are underlings.
Brutus and Cæsar : what should be in that Cæsar ?
Why should that name be sounded more than yours ?
Write them together : yours is as fair a name ;
Sound them, it doth become the mouth as well ;
Weigh them, it is as heavy ; conjure with 'em,

Brutus will start a spirit as soon as Cæsar.
Now, in the names of all the gods at once,
Upon what meat doth this our Cæsar feed
That he is grown so great ?   Age, thou art sham'd.   150
Rome, thou hast lost the breed of noble bloods.
When went there by an age, since the great flood,
But it was fam'd with more than with one man ?
When could they say (till now) that talk'd of Rome,
That her wide walks encompass'd but one man ?
Now is it Rome indeed, and room enough,
When there is in it but one only man.
O, you and I have heard our fathers say,
There was a Brutus once, that would have brook'd
The eternal devil to keep his state in Rome,   160
As easily as a king.

Bru. That you do love me, I am nothing jealous ;
What you would work me to, I have some aim :
How I have thought of this, and of these times,
I shall recount hereafter.   For this present,
I would not so (with love I might entreat you)
Be any further mov'd.   What you have said,
I will consider ; what you have to say
I will with patience hear, and find a time
Both meet to hear, and answer such high things.   170
Till then, my noble friend, chew upon this :

Brutus had rather be a villager,
Than to repute himself a son of Rome
Under these hard conditions, as this time
Is like to lay upon us.

Cas. I am glad that my weak words
Have struck but thus much show of fire from Brutus.

Bru. The games are done, and Cæsar is returning.

Cas. As they pass by, pluck Casca by the sleeve,
And he will (after his sour fashion) tell you   180
What hath proceeded worthy note to-day.

Re-enter Cæsar and his Train

Bru. I will do so : but look you, Cassius,
The angry spot doth glow on Cæsar's brow,
And all the rest look like a chidden train :
Calpurnia's cheek is pale, and Cicero
Looks with such ferret and such fiery eyes
As we have seen him in the Capitol,
Being cross'd in conference by some senators.

Cas. Casca will tell us what the matter is.

Cæs. Antonius !   190

Ant. Cæsar ?

Cæs. Let me have men about me that are fat,
Sleek-headed men, and such as sleep o' nights :
Yond Cassius has a lean and hungry look,
He thinks too much : such men are dangerous.

Ant. Fear him not, Cæsar, he's not dangerous,
    He is a noble Roman, and well given.
Cæs. Would he were fatter ! but I fear him not :
    Yet if my name were liable to fear,
    I do not know the man I should avoid   200
    So soon as that spare Cassius. He reads much,
    He is a great observer, and he looks
    Quite through the deeds of men : he loves no plays,
    As thou dost, Antony ; he hears no music :
    Seldom he smiles, and smiles in such a sort
    As if he mock'd himself, and scorn'd his spirit
    That could be mov'd to smile at any thing.
    Such men as he be never at heart's ease,
    Whiles they behold a greater than themselves,
    And therefore are they very dangerous.   210
    I rather tell thee what is to be fear'd,
    Than what I fear : for always I am Cæsar.
    Come on my right hand, for this ear is deaf,
    And tell me truly, what thou think'st of him.

                Sennet. Exeunt Cæsar and all
                        his Train but Casca

Csc. You pull'd me by the cloak, would you speak with me ?
Bru. Aye, Casca, tell us what hath chanc'd to-day
    That Cæsar looks so sad.
Csc. Why, you were with him, were you not ?

Bru. I should not then ask Casca what had chanc'd.

Csc. Why, there was a crown offer'd him : and being 220
offer'd him, he put it by with the back of his hand,
thus, and then the people fell a-shouting.

Bru. What was the second noise for ?

Csc. Why, for that too.

Cas. They shouted thrice : what was the last cry for ?

Ca. Why, for that too.

Bru. Was the crown offered him thrice ?

Csc. Ay, marry, was 't, and he put it by thrice, every time
gentler than other ; and at every putting by, mine
honest neighbours shouted. 230

Cas. Who offer'd him the crown ?

Csc. Why, Antony.

Bru. Tell us the manner of it, gentle Casca.

Csc. I can as well be hang'd as tell the manner of it : it
was mere foolery ; I did not mark it. I saw Mark
Antony offer him a crown, yet 'twas not a crown
neither, 'twas one of these coronets : and, as I told
you, he put it by once : but for all that, to my
thinking, he would fain have had it. Then he
offer'd it to him again ; then he put it by again : 240
but, to my thinking, he was very loath to lay his
fingers off it. And then he offer'd it the third time ;
he put it the third time by, and still as he refus'd it,

the rabblement hooted, and clapp'd their chopp'd
hands, and threw up their sweaty night-caps, and
uttered such a deal of stinking breath, because Cæsar
refus'd the crown, that it had almost chok'd Cæsar ;
for he swounded, and fell down at it : and for mine
own part, I durst not laugh, for fear of opening my
lips, and receiving the bad air.   250

Cas. But soft, I pray you : what, did Cæsar swound ?

Csc. He fell down in the market-place, and foam'd at
mouth, and was speechless.

Bru. 'Tis very like : he hath the falling-sickness.

Cas. No, Cæsar hath it not : but you, and I,
And honest Casca, we have the falling-sickness.

Csc. I know not what you mean by that, but I am sure
Cæsar fell down.   If the tag-rag people did not clap
him, and hiss him, according as he pleas'd, and dis-
pleas'd them, as they use to do the players in the   260
theatre, I am no true man.

Bru. What said he, when he came unto himself ?

Csc. Marry, before he fell down, when he perceiv'd the
common herd was glad he refus'd the crown, he
pluck'd me ope his doublet, and offer'd them his
throat to cut : an I had been a man of any occupa-   †
tion, if I would not have taken him at a word, I
would I might go to hell among the rogues ; and

so he fell. When he came to himself again, he said,
if he had done or said any thing amiss, he desir'd 270
their worships to think it was his infirmity. Three
or four wenches where I stood, cried, ' Alas, good
soul ! ' and forgave him with all their hearts : but
there 's no heed to be taken of them ; if Cæsar had
stabb'd their mothers, they would have done no less.

Bru. And after that, he came thus sad away ?

Csc. Ay.

Cas. Did Cicero say any thing ?

Csc. Ay, he spoke Greek.

Cas. To what effect ? 280

Csc. Nay, an I tell you that, I 'll ne'er look you i' the face
again : but those that understood him smil'd at one
another, and shook their heads : but for mine own
part, it was Greek to me. I could tell you more
news too : Marullus and Flavius, for pulling scarfs
off Cæsar's images, are put to silence. Fare you
well. There was more foolery yet, if I could
remember it.

Cas. Will you sup with me to-night, Casca ?

Csc. No, I am promis'd forth. 290

Cas. Will you dine with me to-morrow ?

Csc. Ay, if I be alive, and your mind hold, and your
dinner worth the eating.

16

Cas. Good, I will expect you.

Csc. Do so : farewell, both.   *Exit*

Bru. What a blunt fellow is this grown to be !
    He was quick metal when he went to school.

Cas. So is he now, in execution
    Of any bold or noble enterprise,
    However he puts on this tardy form :   300
    This rudeness is a sauce to his good wit,
    Which gives men stomach to digest his words
    With better appetite.

Bru. And so it is.   For this time I will leave you :
    To-morrow, if you please to speak with me,
    I will come home to you ; or, if you will,
    Come home to me, and I will wait for you.

Cas. I will do so : till then, think of the world.

                         Exit Brutus

    Well, Brutus, thou art noble ; yet I see
    Thy honourable metal may be wrought   310
    From that it is dispos'd : therefore, it is meet
    That noble minds keep ever with their likes ;
    For who so firm that cannot be seduc'd ?
    Cæsar doth bear me hard, but he loves Brutus.
    If I were Brutus now, and he were Cassius,
    He should not humour me.   I will this night,
    In several hands, in at his windows throw,

As if they came from several citizens,
Writings, all tending to the great opinion
That Rome holds of his name : wherein obscurely   320
Cæsar's ambition shall be glanced at.
And after this, let Cæsar seat him sure,
For we will shake him, or worse days endure. *Exit*

The night of the same day

*Thunder and Lightning.   Enter, from opposite sides, Casca,
with his sword drawn, and Cicero*

Cic. Good even, Casca : brought you Cæsar home ?
    Why are you breathless, and why stare you so ?
Csc. Are not you mov'd, when all the sway of earth
    Shakes, like a thing unfirm ?   O Cicero,
    I have seen tempests, when the scolding winds
    Have riv'd the knotty oaks, and I have seen
    The ambitious ocean swell, and rage, and foam,
    To be exalted with the threatening clouds :
    But never till to-night, never till now,
    Did I go through a tempest dropping fire.   10
    Either there is a civil strife in heaven,

    Or else the world, too saucy with the gods,
    Incenses them to send destruction.
Cic. Why, saw you any thing more wonderful ?
Csc. A common slave—you know him well by sight—
    Held up his left hand, which did flame and burn
    Like twenty torches join'd ; and yet his hand,
    Not sensible of fire, remain'd unscorch'd.
    Besides—I ha' not since put up my sword—
    Against the Capitol I met a lion,   20
    Who glaz'd upon me, and went surly by,
    Without annoying me : and there were drawn
    Upon a heap a hundred ghastly women,
    Transformed with their fear, who swore, they saw
    Men, all in fire, walk up and down the streets.
    And yesterday the bird of night did sit,
    Even at noon-day, upon the market-place,
    Hooting, and shrieking.   When these prodigies
    Do so conjointly meet, let not men say,
    ' These are their reasons : they are natural : '   30
    For I believe they are portentous things
    Unto the climate that they point upon.
Cic. Indeed, it is a strange-disposed time :
    But men may construe things after their fashion,
    Clean from the purpose of the things themselves.
    Comes Cæsar to the Capitol to-morrow ?

Csc. He doth ; for he did bid Antonius
    Send word to you, he would be there to-morrow.

Cic. Good night then, Casca : this disturbed sky
    Is not to walk in.

Csc.   Farewell, Cicero.   *Exit Cicero*   40
                     Enter Cassius

Cas. Who 's there ?

Csc.   A Roman.

Cas.   Casca, by your voice.

Csc. Your ear is good.   Cassius, what night is this !

Cas. A very pleasing night to honest men.

Csc. Who ever knew the heavens menace so ?

Cas. Those that have known the earth so full of faults.
    For my part, I have walk'd about the streets,
    Submitting me unto the perilous night ;
    And thus unbraced, Casca, as you see,
    Have bar'd my bosom to the thunder-stone ;
    And when the cross blue lightning seem'd to open   50
    The breast of heaven, I did present myself
    Even in the aim and very flash of it.

Csc. But wherefore did you so much tempt the heavens ?
    It is the part of men to fear and tremble
    When the most mighty gods by tokens send
    Such dreadful heralds, to astonish us.

Cas. You are dull, Casca ; and those sparks of life,

That should be in a Roman, you do want,
Or else you use not.   You look pale, and gaze,
And put on fear, and cast yourself in wonder,   60
To see the strange impatience of the heavens :
But if you would consider the true cause,
Why all these fires, why all these gliding ghosts,
Why birds and beasts, from quality and kind,
Why old men, fools, and children calculate,   †
Why all these things change from their ordinance,
Their natures, and preformed faculties,
To monstrous quality ; why, you shall find
That heaven hath infus'd them with these spirits,
To make them instruments of fear, and warning,   70
Unto some monstrous state.
Now could I, Casca, name to thee a man
Most like this dreadful night,
That thunders, lightens, opens graves, and roars,
As doth the lion in the Capitol :
A man no mightier than thyself, or me,
In personal action ; yet prodigious grown,
And fearful, as these strange eruptions are.

Csc. 'Tis Cæsar that you mean ; is it not, Cassius ?

Cas. Let it be who it is : for Romans now   80
Have thews and limbs, like to their ancestors ;
But, woe the while ! our fathers' minds are dead,

21

And we are govern'd with our mothers' spirits,
Our yoke, and sufferance, show us womanish.

Csc. Indeed, they say, the senators to-morrow
Mean to establish Cæsar as a king;
And he shall wear his crown by sea, and land,
In every place, save here in Italy.

Cas. I know where I will wear this dagger then:
Cassius from bondage will deliver Cassius: 90
Therein, ye gods, you make the weak most strong;
Therein, ye gods, you tyrants do defeat:
Nor stony tower, nor walls of beaten brass,
Nor airless dungeon, nor strong links of iron,
Can be retentive to the strength of spirit;
But life, being weary of these worldly bars,
Never lacks power to dismiss itself.
If I know this, know all the world besides,
That part of tyranny that I do bear
I can shake off at pleasure. *Thunder still*

Csc.   So can I: 100
So every bondman in his own hand bears
The power to cancel his captivity.

Cas. And why should Cæsar be a tyrant then?
Poor man, I know he would not be a wolf,
But that he sees the Romans are but sheep:
He were no lion, were not Romans hinds.

Those that with haste will make a mighty fire,
Begin it with weak straws : what trash is Rome,
What rubbish and what offal ? when it serves
For the base matter, to illuminate 110
So vile a thing as Cæsar. But, O grief,
Where hast thou led me ? I perhaps speak this
Before a willing bondman ; then I know
My answer must be made. But I am arm'd,
And dangers are to me indifferent.

Csc. You speak to Casca, and to such a man
That is no fleering tell-tale. Hold, my hand :
Be factious for redress of all these griefs,
And I will set this foot of mine as far
As who goes farthest.

Cas. There 's a bargain made. 120
Now know you, Casca, I have mov'd already
Some certain of the noblest-minded Romans
To undergo, with me, an enterprise
Of honourable-dangerous consequence ;
And I do know, by this they stay for me
In Pompey's porch : for now, this fearful night,
There is no stir, or walking in the streets ;
And the complexion of the element
In favour 's like the work we have in hand,
Most bloody, fiery, and most terrible. 130

Enter Cinna

Csc. Stand close awhile, for here comes one in haste.

Cas. 'Tis Cinna, I do know him by his gait,
    He is a friend.   Cinna, where haste you so ?

Cin. To find out you.   Who's that ? Metellus Cimber ?

Cas. No, it is Casca ; one incorporate
    To our attempts.   Am I not stay'd for, Cinna ?

Cin. I am glad on 't.   What a fearful night is this !
    There's two or three of us have seen strange sights.

Cas. Am I not stay'd for ? tell me.

Cin.   Yes, you are.
    O Cassius, if you could   140
    But win the noble Brutus to our party—

Cas. Be you content.   Good Cinna, take this paper,
    And look you lay it in the prætor's chair,
    Where Brutus may but find it : and throw this
    In at his window ; set this up with wax
    Upon old Brutus' statue : all this done,
    Repair to Pompey's porch, where you shall find us.
    Is Decius Brutus and Trebonius there ?

Cin. All, but Metellus Cimber, and he's gone
    To seek you at your house.   Well, I will hie,   150
    And so bestow these papers as you bade me.

Cas. That done, repair to Pompey's theatre.   *Exit Cinna*
    Come, Casca, you and I will yet, ere day,

See Brutus at his house : three parts of him
Is ours already, and the man entire
Upon the next encounter yields him ours.

Csc. O, he sits high in all the people's hearts ;
And that which would appear offence in us,
His countenance, like richest alchemy,
Will change to virtue, and to worthiness.　　　160

Cas. Him, and his worth, and our great need of him,
You have right well conceited : let us go,
For it is after midnight, and ere day
We will awake him, and be sure of him.　　*Exeunt*

Act Second

SCENE I

Between 2 and 3 a.m. of the same night

Brutus's Orchard

Enter Brutus

Bru. What, Lucius, ho !
I cannot, by the progress of the stars,
Give guess how near to day.　Lucius, I say !
I would it were my fault to sleep so soundly.

When, Lucius, when? awake, I say! what, Lucius!

Enter Lucius

Luc. Call'd you, my lord?

Bru. Get me a taper in my study, Lucius:

When it is lighted, come and call me here.

Luc. I will, my lord.   *Exit*

Bru. It must be by his death: and, for my part,   10

I know no personal cause to spurn at him,

But for the general.   He would be crown'd:

How that might change his nature, there's the question.

It is the bright day that brings forth the adder;

And that craves wary walking: crown him?—that?—

And then, I grant, we put a sting in him,

That at his will he may do danger with.

The abuse of greatness is when it disjoins

Remorse from power: and, to speak truth of Cæsar,

I have not known when his affections sway'd   20

More than his reason.   But 'tis a common proof,

That lowliness is young ambition's ladder,

Whereto the climber upward turns his face;

But when he once attains the upmost round,

He then unto the ladder turns his back,

Looks in the clouds, scorning the base degrees

By which he did ascend: so Cæsar may;

Then, lest he may, prevent.   And, since the quarrel

Will bear no colour for the thing he is,
Fashion it thus ; that what he is, augmented,   30
Would run to these and these extremities :
And therefore think him as a serpent's egg,
Which, hatch'd, would as his kind grow mischievous ;
And kill him in the shell.

Re-enter Lucius

Luc. The taper burneth in your closet, sir :
Searching the window for a flint, I found
This paper, thus seal'd up, and I am sure
It did not lie there when I went to bed.

Gives him the letter

Bru. Get you to bed again, it is not day :
Is not to-morrow, boy, the ides of March ?   40
Luc. I know not, sir.
Bru. Look in the calendar and bring me word.
Luc. I will, sir.   *Exit*
Bru. The exhalations, whizzing in the air,
Give so much light, that I may read by them.

Opens the letter and reads

' Brutus, thou sleep'st : awake, and see thyself :
Shall Rome, &c.   Speak, strike, redress.'
' Brutus, thou sleep'st : awake.'
Such instigations have been often dropp'd
Where I have took them up :   50

'Shall Rome, &c.' Thus must I piece it out:
Shall Rome stand under one man's awe? What
    Rome?
My ancestors did from the streets of Rome
The Tarquin drive, when he was call'd a king.
'Speak, strike, redress.' Am I entreated
To speak, and strike? O Rome, I make thee promise,
If the redress will follow, thou receivest
Thy full petition at the hand of Brutus!

Re-enter Lucius

Luc. Sir, March is wasted fifteen days.   *Knocking within*
Bru. 'Tis good. Go to the gate; somebody knocks.   60

Exit Lucius

Since Cassius first did whet me against Cæsar
I have not slept.
Between the acting of a dreadful thing
And the first motion, all the interim is
Like a phantasma, or a hideous dream:
The Genius, and the mortal instruments
Are then in council; and the state of a man,
Like to a little kingdom, suffers then
The nature of an insurrection.

Re-enter Lucius

Luc. Sir, 'tis your brother Cassius at the door,   70
Who doth desire to see you.

28

Bru.   Is he alone ?

Luc. No, sir, there are moe with him.

Bru.   Do you know them ?

Luc. No, sir, their hats are pluck'd about their ears,
And half their faces buried in their cloaks,
That by no means I may discover them,
By any mark of favour.

Bru.   Let 'em enter :   *Exit Lucius*
They are the faction.   O conspiracy,
Sham'st thou to show thy dangerous brow by night,
When evils are most free ?   O then, by day
Where wilt thou find a cavern dark enough   80
To mask thy monstrous visage ?   Seek none,
      conspiracy,
Hide it in smiles and affability :
For if thou put thy native semblance on,   †
Not Erebus itself were dim enough
To hide thee from prevention.
      Enter the conspirators, Cassius, Casca, Decius, Cinna,
            Metellus Cimber, and Trebonius

Cas. I think we are too bold upon your rest :
Good morrow, Brutus, do we trouble you ?

Bru. I have been up this hour, awake all night :
Know I these men that come along with you ?

Cas. Yes, every man of them ; and no man here   90

But honours you ; and every one doth wish
You had but that opinion of yourself
Which every noble Roman bears of you.
This is Trebonius.

Bru.　　　　　　　He is welcome hither.

Cas. This, Decius Brutus.

Bru.　　　　　　He is welcome too.

Cas. This, Casca ; this, Cinna ; and this, Metellus Cimber.

Bru. They are all welcome.
What watchful cares do interpose themselves
Betwixt your eyes and night ?

Cas. Shall I entreat a word ?　　　　*They whisper*　100

Dec. Here lies the east : doth not the day break here ?

Csc. No.

Cin. O, pardon, sir, it doth ; and yon grey lines,
That fret the clouds, are messengers of day.

Csc. You shall confess that you are both deceiv'd :
Here, as I point my sword, the sun arises,
Which is a great way growing on the south,
Weighing the youthful season of the year.
Some two months hence, up higher toward the north
He first presents his fire, and the high east　　110
Stands as the Capitol, directly here.

Bru. Give me your hands all over, one by one.

Cas. And let us swear our resolution.

Bru. No, not an oath : if not the face of men,   †
    The sufferance of our souls, the time's abuse,—
    If these be motives weak, break off betimes,
    And every man hence, to his idle bed ;
    So let high-sighted tyranny range on,
    Till each man drop by lottery.   But if these
    (As I am sure they do) bear fire enough   120
    To kindle cowards, and to steel with valour
    The melting spirits of women ; then, countrymen,
    What need we any spur, but our own cause
    To prick us to redress ? what other bond,
    Than secret Romans, that have spoke the word,
    And will not palter ? and what other oath,
    Than honesty to honesty engag'd,
    That this shall be, or we will fall for it ?
    Swear priests and cowards and men cautelous,
    Old feeble carrions, and such suffering souls   130
    That welcome wrongs ; unto bad causes swear
    Such creatures as men doubt ; but do not stain
    The even virtue of our enterprise,
    Nor the insuppressive mettle of our spirits,
    To think, that or our cause, or our performance
    Did need an oath.   When every drop of blood
    That every Roman bears, and nobly bears,
    Is guilty of a several bastardy,

31

If he do break the smallest particle
Of any promise that hath pass'd from him.   140
Cas. But what of Cicero ? shall we sound him ?
    I think he will stand very strong with us.
Csc. Let us not leave him out.
Cin.   No, by no means.
Met. O, let us have him, for his silver hairs
    Will purchase us a good opinion,
    And buy men's voices, to commend our deeds :
    It shall be said his judgment rul'd our hands,
    Our youths, and wildness, shall no whit appear,
    But all be buried in his gravity.
Bru. O, name him not ; let us not break with him,   150
    For he will never follow any thing
    That other men begin.
Cas.   Then leave him out.
Csc. Indeed, he is not fit.
Dec. Shall no man else be touch'd, but only Cæsar ?
Cas. Decius, well urg'd : I think it is not meet
    Mark Antony, so well belov'd of Cæsar,
    Should outlive Cæsar ; we shall find of him
    A shrewd contriver : and you know, his means,
    If he improve them, may well stretch so far
    As to annoy us all : which to prevent,   160
    Let Antony and Cæsar fall together.

Bru. Our course will seem too bloody, Caius Cassius,
    To cut the head off, and then hack the limbs ;
    Like wrath in death, and envy afterwards :
    For Antony is but a limb of Cæsar.
    Let us be sacrificers, but not butchers, Caius :
    We all stand up against the spirit of Cæsar,
    And in the spirit of men there is no blood :
    O, that we then could come by Cæsar's spirit,
    And not dismember Cæsar ! But (alas)   170
    Cæsar must bleed for it. And, gentle friends,
    Let 's kill him boldly, but not wrathfully ;
    Let 's carve him, as a dish fit for the gods,
    Not hew him as a carcass fit for hounds :
    And let our hearts, as subtle masters do,
    Stir up their servants to an act of rage,
    And after seem to chide 'em. This shall make
    Our purpose necessary, and not envious :
    Which so appearing to the common eyes,
    We shall be call'd purgers, not murderers.   180
    And for Mark Antony, think not of him ;
    For he can do no more than Cæsar's arm,
    When Cæsar's head is off.
Cas.   Yet I fear him,
    For in the ingrafted love he bears to Cæsar—
Bru. Alas, good Cassius, do not think of him :

33

      If he love Cæsar, all that he can do
      Is to himself ; take thought and die for Cæsar,
      And that were much he should ; for he is given
      To sports, to wildness, and much company.

Tre. There is no fear in him ; let him not die,   190
      For he will live, and laugh at this hereafter.

                            Clock strikes

Bru. Peace ! count the clock.

Cas.   The clock hath stricken three.

Tre. 'Tis time to part.

Cas.   But it is doubtful yet
      Whether Cæsar will come forth to-day, or no :
      For he is superstitious grown of late,
      Quite from the main opinion he held once,
      Of fantasy, of dreams, and ceremonies :
      It may be, these apparent prodigies,
      The unaccustom'd terror of this night,
      And the persuasion of his augurers,   200
      May hold him from the Capitol to-day.

Dec. Never fear that : if he be so resolv'd,
      I can o'ersway him ; for he loves to hear
      That unicorns may be betray'd with trees,
      And bears with glasses, elephants with holes,
      Lions with toils, and men with flatterers :
      But, when I tell him he hates flatterers,

He says he does ; being then most flattered.
Let me work ;
For I can give his humour the true bent ;   210
And I will bring him to the Capitol.

Cas. Nay, we will all of us be there to fetch him.

Bru. By the eighth hour, is that the uttermost ?

Cin. Be that the uttermost, and fail not then.

Met. Caius Ligarius doth bear Cæsar hard,
Who rated him for speaking well of Pompey ;
I wonder none of you have thought of him.

Bru. Now, good Metellus, go along by him :
He loves me well, and I have given him reasons,
Send him but hither, and I 'll fashion him.   220

Cas. The morning comes upon 's : we 'll leave you, Brutus,
And, friends, disperse yourselves ; but all remember
What you have said, and show yourselves true Romans.

Bru. Good gentlemen, look fresh and merrily,
Let not our looks put on our purposes ;
But bear it as our Roman actors do,
With untir'd spirits, and formal constancy,
And so good morrow to you every one.

Exeunt all but Brutus

Boy ! Lucius ! Fast asleep ? It is no matter,
Enjoy the honey-heavy dew of slumber :   230
Thou hast no figures, nor no fantasies,

Which busy care draws in the brains of men ;
Therefore thou sleep'st so sound.

Enter Portia

Por.   Brutus, my lord !

Bru. Portia ; what mean you ? wherefore rise you now ?
It is not for your health, thus to commit
Your weak condition to the raw cold morning.

Por. Nor for yours neither.   You've ungently, Brutus,
Stole from my bed : and yesternight at supper
You suddenly arose, and walk'd about,
Musing, and sighing, with your arms across ;   240
And when I ask'd you what the matter was,
You star'd upon me, with ungentle looks :
I urg'd you further, then you scratch'd your head,
And too impatiently stamp'd with your foot :
Yet I insisted, yet you answer'd not,
But with an angry wafture of your hand
Gave sign for me to leave you : so I did,
Fearing to strengthen that impatience
Which seem'd too much enkindled ; and withal
Hoping it was but an effect of humour,   250
Which sometime hath his hour with every man.
It will not let you eat, nor talk, nor sleep ;
And could it work so much upon your shape,
As it hath much prevail'd on your condition,

I should not know you Brutus.   Dear my lord,
Make me acquainted with your cause of grief.
Bru. I am not well in health, and that is all.
Por. Brutus is wise, and, were he not in health,
He would embrace the means to come by it.
Bru. Why, so I do : good Portia, go to bed.   260
Por. Is Brutus sick ?   and is it physical
    To walk unbraced, and suck up the humours
    Of the dank morning ?   What, is Brutus sick ?
    And will he steal out of his wholesome bed,
    To dare the vile contagion of the night ?
    And tempt the rheumy and unpurged air
    To add unto his sickness ?   No, my Brutus,
    You have some sick offence within your mind,
    Which by the right and virtue of my place
    I ought to know of : and, upon my knees,   270
    I charm you, by my once commended beauty,
    By all your vows of love, and that great vow
    Which did incorporate and make us one,
    That you unfold to me, your self, your half,
    Why you are heavy ; and what men to-night
    Have had resort to you ; for here have been
    Some six or seven, who did hide their faces
    Even from darkness.
Bru.   Kneel not, gentle Portia.

37

Por. I should not need, if you were gentle Brutus.
 Within the bond of marriage, tell me, Brutus,   280
 Is it excepted, I should know no secrets
 That appertain to you ?   Am I yourself
 But as it were in sort, or limitation ?
 To keep with you at meals, comfort your bed,
 And talk to you sometimes ?   Dwell I but in the   †
  suburbs
 Of your good pleasure ?   If it be no more,
 Portia is Brutus' harlot, not his wife.
Bru. You are my true and honourable wife,
 As dear to me as are the ruddy drops
 That visit my sad heart.   290
Por. If this were true, then should I know this secret.
 I grant I am a woman ; but withal,
 A woman that Lord Brutus took to wife :
 I grant I am a woman ; but withal,
 A woman well reputed ; Cato's daughter.
 Think you I am no stronger than my sex,
 Being so father'd, and so husbanded ?
 Tell me your counsels, I will not disclose 'em :
 I have made strong proof of my constancy,
 Giving myself a voluntary wound   300
 Here, in the thigh : can I bear that with patience,
 And not my husband's secrets ?

Bru.   O ye gods !
    Render me worthy of this noble wife ?

Knocking within

    Hark, hark, one knocks : Portia, go in a while,
    And by and by thy bosom shall partake
    The secrets of my heart :
    All my engagements I will construe to thee,
    All the charactery of my sad brows :
    Leave me with haste.   (*exit Portia.*)   Lucius, who 's
       that knocks ?

Re-enter Lucius with Ligarius

Luc. Here is a sick man that would speak with you.   310
Bru. Caius Ligarius, that Metellus spake of.
    Boy, stand aside.   Caius Ligarius, how ?
Lig. Vouchsafe good morrow from a feeble tongue.
Bru. O, what a time have you chose out, brave Caius,
    To wear a kerchief !   Would you were not sick !
Lig. I am not sick, if Brutus have in hand
    Any exploit worthy the name of honour.
Bru. Such an exploit have I in hand, Ligarius,
    Had you a healthful ear to hear of it.
Lig. By all the gods that Romans bow before,   320
    I here discard my sickness.   Soul of Rome,
    Brave son, deriv'd from honourable loins,
    Thou, like an exorcist, hast conjur'd up

  My mortified spirit. Now bid me run,
  And I will strive with things impossible,
  Yea, get the better of them. What 's to do ?
Bru. A piece of work that will make sick men whole.
Lig. But are not some whole that we must make sick ?
Bru. That must we also. What it is, my Caius,
  I shall unfold to thee, as we are going   330
  To whom it must be done.
Lig.   Set on your foot,
  And with a heart new-fir'd I follow you,
  To do I know not what : but it sufficeth
  That Brutus leads me on.   *Thunder*
Bru.   Follow me then. *Exeunt*

SCENE II

The early morning

Cæsar's house

Thunder and lightning. Enter Cæsar, in his night-gown

Cæs. Nor heaven, nor earth, have been at peace to-night :
  Thrice hath Calpurnia in her sleep cried out,
  ' Help, ho ! they murder Cæsar ! ' Who 's within ?
       Enter a Servant
Ser. My Lord.

Cæs. Go bid the priests do present sacrifice,
    And bring me their opinions of success.
Ser. I will, my lord.   *Exit*

Enter Calpurnia

Cal. What mean you, Cæsar ? think you to walk forth ?
    You shall not stir out of your house to-day.
Cæs. Cæsar shall forth ; the things that threaten'd me   10
    Ne'er look'd but on my back : when they shall see
    The face of Cæsar, they are vanished.
Cal. Cæsar, I never stood on ceremonies,
    Yet now they fright me : there is one within,
    Besides the things that we have heard and seen,
    Recounts most horrid sights seen by the watch.
    A lioness hath whelped in the streets,
    And graves have yawn'd, and yielded up their dead ;
    Fierce fiery warriors fight upon the clouds
    In ranks and squadrons and right form of war,   20
    Which drizzled blood upon the Capitol ;
    The noise of battle hurtled in the air ;
    Horses did neigh, and dying men did groan,
    And ghosts did shriek and squeal about the streets.
    O Cæsar, these things are beyond all use,
    And I do fear them.
Cæs.   What can be avoided
    Whose end is purpos'd by the mighty gods ?

     Yet Cæsar shall go forth ; for these predictions
     Are to the world in general as to Cæsar.

Cal. When beggars die, there are no comets seen,   30
     The heavens themselves blaze forth the death of
        princes.

Cæs. Cowards die many times before their death,
     The valiant never taste of death but once :
     Of all the wonders that I yet have heard,
     It seems to me most strange that men should fear,
     Seeing that death, a necessary end,
     Will come when it will come.

               Re-enter Servant

              What say the augurers ?

Ser. They would not have you to stir forth to-day.
     Plucking the entrails of an offering forth,
     They could not find a heart within the beast.   40

Cæs. The gods do this in shame of cowardice :
     Cæsar should be a beast without a heart
     If he should stay at home to-day for fear :
     No, Cæsar shall not : danger knows full well
     That Cæsar is more dangerous than he :
     We are two lions litter'd in one day,   †
     And I the elder and more terrible,
     And Cæsar shall go forth.

Cal.   Alas, my lord,

    Your wisdom is consum'd in confidence:
    Do not go forth to-day: call it my fear,   50
    That keeps you in the house, and not your own.
    We'll send Mark Antony to the senate-house,
    And he shall say you are not well to-day:
    Let me, upon my knee, prevail in this.

Cæs. Mark Antony shall say I am not well,
    And, for thy humour, I will stay at home.

               Enter Decius

    Here's Decius Brutus, he shall tell them so.

Dec. Cæsar, all hail! good-morrow, worthy Cæsar,
    I come to fetch you to the senate-house.

Cæs. And you are come in very happy time,   60
    To bear my greeting to the senators,
    And tell them that I will not come to-day:
    Cannot, is false; and that I dare not, falser:
    I will not come to-day, tell them so, Decius.

Cal. Say he is sick.

Cæs.   Shall Cæsar send a lie?
    Have I in conquest stretch'd mine arm so far,
    To be afear'd to tell graybeards the truth?
    Decius, go tell them, Cæsar will not come.

Dec. Most mighty Cæsar, let me know some cause,
    Lest I be laugh'd at when I tell them so.   70

Cæs. The cause is in my will, I will not come,

That is enough to satisfy the senate.
But, for your private satisfaction,
Because I love you, I will let you know.
Calpurnia here, my wife, stays me at home:
She dreamt to-night she saw my statuë,
Which, like a fountain, with an hundred spouts
Did run pure blood; and many lusty Romans
Came smiling, and did bathe their hands in it:
And these does she apply, for warnings and portents   80
And evils imminent; and on her knee
Hath begg'd, that I will stay at home to-day.

Dec. This dream is all amiss interpreted,
It was a vision fair and fortunate:
Your statue spouting blood in many pipes,
In which so many smiling Romans bath'd,
Signifies that from you great Rome shall suck
Reviving blood, and that great men shall press
For tinctures, stains, relics, and cognizance.   †
This by Calpurnia's dream is signified.   90

Cæs. And this way have you well expounded it.

Dec. I have, when you have heard what I can say:
And know it now, the senate have concluded
To give this day a crown to mighty Cæsar.
If you shall send them word you will not come,
Their minds may change. Besides, it were a mock

44

Apt to be render'd, for some one to say,
' Break up the senate till another time ;
When Cæsar's wife shall meet with better dreams.'
If Cæsar hide himself, shall they not whisper   100
' Lo, Cæsar is afraid ' ?
Pardon me, Cæsar, for my dear dear love
To your proceeding bids me tell you this ;
And reason to my love is liable.

Cæs. How foolish do your fears seem now, Calpurnia !
I am ashamed I did yield to them.
Give me my robe, for I will go.

> *Enter Publius, Brutus, Ligarius, Metellus, Casca,*
> *Trebonius, and Cinna*

And look where Publius is come to fetch me.

Pub. Good morrow, Cæsar.

Cæs.   Welcome, Publius.
What, Brutus, are you stirr'd so early too ?   110
Good morrow, Casca : Caius Ligarius,
Cæsar was ne'er so much your enemy
As that same ague which hath made you lean.
What is 't o'clock ?

Bru.   Cæsar, 'tis strucken eight.

Cæs. I thank you for your pains and courtesy.

> *Enter Antony*

See, Antony, that revels long o' nights,

Is notwithstanding up. Good morrow, Antony.

Ant. So to most noble Cæsar.

Cæs.   Bid them prepare within :
I am to blame to be thus waited for.
Now, Cinna, now, Metellus : what, Trebonius !   120
I have an hour's talk in store for you ;
Remember that you call on me to-day :
Be near me, that I may remember you.

Tre. Cæsar, I will : *(aside)* and so near will I be,
That your best friends shall wish I had been further.

Cæs. Good friends, go in, and taste some wine with me ;
And we (like friends) will straightway go together.

Bru. (aside) That every like is not the same, O Cæsar,
The heart of Brutus yearns to think upon !   *Exeunt*

SCENES III AND **IV**

About an hour later

A street

Enter Artemidorus, reading a paper

Art. ' Cæsar, beware of Brutus, take heed of Cassius ;
come not near Casca, have an eye to Cinna, trust not
Trebonius, mark well Metellus Cimber, Decius
Brutus loves thee not : thou hast wronged Caius

Ligarius.   There is but one mind in all these men, and it is bent against Cæsar. If thou beest not immortal, look about you : security gives way to conspiracy.   The mighty gods defend thee !

Thy lover, ARTEMIDORUS.'

Here will I stand, till Cæsar pass along,   10
And as a suitor will I give him this :
My heart laments that virtue cannot live
Out of the teeth of emulation.
If thou read this, O Cæsar, thou mayest live ;
If not, the Fates with traitors do contrive.   *Exit*

Enter Portia and Lucius

Por. I prithee, boy, run to the senate-house,
       Stay not to answer me, but get thee gone.
       Why dost thou stay ?
Luc.   To know my errand, madam.
Por. I would have had thee there and here again
       Ere I can tell thee what thou shouldst do there :
       O constancy, be strong upon my side,
       Set a huge mountain 'tween my heart and tongue :

    I have a man's mind, but a woman's might:
How hard it is for women to keep counsel!
Art thou here yet?

Luc.   Madam, what should I do?   10
Run to the Capitol, and nothing else?
And so return to you, and nothing else?

Por. Yes, bring me word, boy, if thy lord look well,
For he went sickly forth: and take good note
What Cæsar doth, what suitors press to him.
Hark, boy, what noise is that?

Luc. I hear none, madam.

Por.   Prithee, listen well:
I heard a bustling rumour like a fray,
And the wind brings it from the Capitol.

Luc. Sooth, madam, I hear nothing.

            Enter the Soothsayer

Por.   Come hither, fellow: 20
Which way hast thou been?

Soo.   At mine own house, good lady.

Por. What is 't o'clock?

Soo.   About the ninth hour, lady.   †

Por. Is Cæsar yet gone to the Capitol?

Soo. Madam, not yet: I go to take my stand,
To see him pass on to the Capitol.

Por. Thou hast some suit to Cæsar, hast thou not?

Soo. That I have, lady, if it will please Cæsar
    To be so good to Cæsar as to hear me :
    I shall beseech him to befriend himself.
Por. Why, know'st thou any harm's intended towards him ? 30
Soo. None that I know will be, much that I fear may chance.
    Good morrow to you : here the street is narrow :
    The throng that follows Cæsar at the heels,
    Of senators, of prætors, common suitors,
    Will crowd a feeble man almost to death :
    I 'll get me to a place more void, and there
    Speak to great Cæsar as he comes along.   *Exit*
Por. I must go in.   Ay me ! how weak a thing
    The heart of woman is !   O Brutus,
    The heavens speed thee in thine enterprise !   40
    Sure, the boy heard me :   Brutus hath a suit
    That Cæsar will not grant.   O, I grow faint :
    Run, Lucius, and commend me to my lord,
    Say I am merry ; come to me again,
    And bring me word what he doth say to thee.

                             Exeunt severally

Act Third

SCENE I

A little later

*The Senate sitting. A crowd waiting; among them
Artemidorus and the Soothsayer*

*Flourish. Enter Cæsar, Brutus, Cassius, Casca, Decius,
Metellus, Trebonius, Cinna, Antony, Lepidus, Popilius,
Publius, and others*

Cæs. The ides of March are come.

Soo. Ay, Cæsar, but not gone.

Art. Hail, Cæsar! read this schedule.

Dec. Trebonius doth desire you to o'er-read
  (At your best leisure) this his humble suit.

Art. O Cæsar, read mine first: for mine's a suit
  That touches Cæsar nearer. Read it, great Cæsar.

Cæs. What touches us ourself shall be last serv'd.

Art. Delay not, Cæsar, read it instantly.

Cæs. What, is the fellow mad?

Pub.   Sirrah, give place.   10

Cas. What, urge you your petitions in the street?
  Come to the Capitol.

Cæsar takes his place, the rest following

Pop. I wish your enterprise to-day may thrive.

Cas. What enterprise, Popilius ?

Pop.   Fare you well.

Advances to Cæsar

Bru. What said Popilius Lena ?

Cas. He wish'd to-day our enterprise might thrive.
I fear our purpose is discovered.

Bru. Look, how he makes to Cæsar : mark him.

Cas.   Casca,
Be sudden, for we fear prevention.
Brutus, what shall be done ?   If this be known,   20
Cassius or Cæsar never shall turn back,
For I will slay myself.

Bru.   Cassius, be constant :
Popilius Lena speaks not of our purposes,
For, look, he smiles, and Cæsar doth not change.

Cas. Trebonius knows his time ; for, look you, Brutus,
He draws Mark Antony out of the way.

Exeunt Antony and Trebonius

Dec. Where is Metellus Cimber ?   Let him go,
And presently prefer his suit to Cæsar.

Bru. He is address'd : press near, and second him.

Cin. Casca, you are the first that rears your hand.   30

Cæs. Are we all ready ?   What is now amiss

       That Cæsar and his senate must redress ?

Met. Most high, most mighty, and most puissant Cæsar,
       Metellus Cimber throws before thy seat
       An humble heart :—   *Kneeling*

Cæs.   I must prevent thee, Cimber.
       These couchings, and these lowly courtesies,
       Might fire the blood of ordinary men,
       And turn pre-ordinance, and first decree
       Into the law of children.   Be not fond,   †
       To think that Cæsar bears such rebel blood   40
       That will be thaw'd from the true quality
       With that which melteth fools, I mean, sweet words,
       Low-crooked court'sies and base spaniel-fawning :
       Thy brother by decree is banished :
       If thou dost bend, and pray, and fawn for him,
       I spurn thee like a cur out of my way :
       Know, Cæsar doth not wrong, nor without cause   †
       Will he be satisfied.

Met. Is there no voice more worthy than my own,
       To sound more sweetly in great Cæsar's ear   50
       For the repealing of my banish'd brother ?

Bru. I kiss thy hand, but not in flattery, Cæsar :
       Desiring thee, that Publius Cimber may
       Have an immediate freedom of repeal.

Cæs. What, Brutus ?

Cas.   Pardon, Cæsar; Cæsar, pardon:
As low as to thy foot doth Cassius fall,
To beg enfranchisement for Publius Cimber.
Cæs. I could be well mov'd, if I were as you;
If I could pray to move, prayers would move me:
But I am constant as the northern star,   60
Of whose true-fix'd and resting quality
There is no fellow in the firmament.
The skies are painted with unnumber'd sparks,
They are all fire, and every one doth shine;
But, there's but one in all doth hold his place.
So, in the world; 'tis furnish'd well with men,
And men are flesh and blood, and apprehensive;
Yet in the number, I do know but one
That unassailable holds on his rank,
Unshak'd of motion: and that I am he,   70
Let me a little show it, even in this;
That I was constant Cimber should be banish'd,
And constant do remain to keep him so.
Cin. O Cæsar,—
Cæs.   Hence! wilt thou lift up Olympus?
Dec. Great Cæsar,—
Cæs.   Doth not Brutus bootless kneel?
Csc. Speak, hands, for me!   *They stab Cæsar*
Cæs. Et tu, Brute? Then fall, Cæsar!   *Dies*

Cin. Liberty, freedom ! Tyranny is dead,
    Run hence, proclaim, cry it about the streets.

Cas. Some to the common pulpits, and cry out   80
    ' Liberty, freedom, and enfranchisement ! '

Bru. People and senators, be not affrighted ;
    Fly not, stand still : ambition's debt is paid.

Csc. Go to the pulpit, Brutus.

Dec. And Cassius too.

Bru. Where 's Publius ?

Cin. Here, quite confounded with this mutiny.

Met. Stand fast together, lest some friend of Cæsar's
    Should chance—

Bru. Talk not of standing. Publius, good cheer ;   90
    There is no harm intended to your person,
    Nor to no Roman else : so tell them, Publius.

Cas. And leave us, Publius, lest that the people
    Rushing on us, should do your age some mischief.

Bru. Do so, and let no man abide this deed,
    But we the doers.

             Re-enter Trebonius

Cas. Where is Antony ?

Tre.   Fled to his house amaz'd :
    Men, wives, and children stare, cry out, and run,
    As it were doomsday.

Bru.   Fates, we will know your pleasures :

That we shall die, we know, 'tis but the time,   100
And drawing days out, that men stand upon.

Cas. Why, he that cuts off twenty years of life,
Cuts off so many years of fearing death.

Bru. Grant that, and then is death a benefit :
So are we Cæsar's friends, that have abridg'd
His time of fearing death.   Stoop, Romans, stoop,
And let us bathe our hands in Cæsar's blood
Up to the elbows, and besmear our swords :
Then walk we forth, even to the market-place,
And waving our red weapons o'er our heads,   110
Let 's all cry ' Peace, freedom, and liberty ! '

Cas. Stoop then, and wash.   How many ages hence
Shall this our lofty scene be acted over,
In state unborn, and accents yet unknown !

Bru. How many times shall Cæsar bleed in sport,
That now on Pompey's basis lies along
No worthier than the dust !

Cas.   So oft as that shall be,
So often shall the knot of us be call'd
The men that gave their country liberty.

Dec. What, shall we forth ?

Cas.   Ay, every man away.   120
Brutus shall lead, and we will grace his heels
With the most boldest and best hearts of Rome.

55

Enter a Servant

Bru. Soft, who comes here ? A friend of Antony's.

Ser. Thus, Brutus, did my master bid me kneel ;
   Thus did Mark Antony bid me fall down,
   And, being prostrate, thus he bade me say :
   Brutus is noble, wise, valiant, and honest ;
   Cæsar was mighty, bold, royal, and loving :
   Say, I love Brutus, and I honour him ;
   Say, I fear'd Cæsar, honour'd him, and lov'd him.   130
   If Brutus will vouchsafe that Antony
   May safely come to him, and be resolv'd
   How Cæsar hath deserv'd to lie in death,
   Mark Antony shall not love Cæsar dead
   So well as Brutus living ; but will follow
   The fortunes and affairs of noble Brutus,
   Thorough the hazards of this untrod state,
   With all true faith. So says my master Antony.

Bru. Thy master is a wise and valiant Roman,
   I never thought him worse :   140
   Tell him, so please him come unto this place,
   He shall be satisfied ; and, by my honour,
   Depart untouch'd.

Ser.   I 'll fetch him presently.   *Exit*

Bru. I know that we shall have him well to friend.

Cas. I wish we may : but yet have I a mind

That fears him much ; and my misgiving still
Falls shrewdly to the purpose.

Re-enter Antony

Bru. But here comes Antony.   Welcome, Mark Antony.

Ant. O mighty Cæsar ! dost thou lie so low ?
    Are all thy conquests, glories, triumphs, spoils,   150
    Shrunk to this little measure ?   Fare thee well.
    I know not, gentlemen, what you intend,
    Who else must be let blood, who else is rank :
    If I myself, there is no hour so fit
    As Cæsar's death's hour ; nor no instrument
    Of half that worth as those your swords ; made rich
    With the most noble blood of all this world.
    I do beseech ye, if you bear me hard,
    Now, whilst your purpled hands do reek and smoke,
    Fulfil your pleasure.   Live a thousand years,   160
    I shall not find myself so apt to die :
    No place will please me so, no mean of death,
    As here by Cæsar, and by you cut off,
    The choice and master spirits of this age.

Bru. O Antony ! beg not your death of us :
    Though now we must appear bloody and cruel,
    As by our hands, and this our present act,
    You see we do ; yet see you but our hands,
    And this, the bleeding business they have done :

Our hearts you see not, they are pitiful :   170
And pity to the general wrong of Rome—   †
As fire drives out fire, so pity pity—
Hath done this deed on Cæsar.   For your part,
To you our swords have leaden points, Mark Antony :
Our arms in strength of malice, and our hearts   †
Of brothers' temper, do receive you in,
With all kind love, good thoughts, and reverence.

Cas. Your voice shall be as strong as any man's,
In the disposing of new dignities.

Bru. Only be patient, till we have appeas'd   180
The multitude, beside themselves with fear,
And then, we will deliver you the cause,
Why I, that did love Cæsar when I struck him,
Have thus proceeded.

Ant.   I doubt not of your wisdom :
Let each man render me his bloody hand.
First, Marcus Brutus, will I shake with you ;
Next, Caius Cassius, do I take your hand ;
Now, Decius Brutus, yours ; now yours, Metellus ;
Yours, Cinna ; and, my valiant Casca, yours ;
Though last, not least in love, yours, good Trebonius.
Gentlemen all,—alas, what shall I say ?   191
My credit now stands on such slippery ground,
That one of two bad ways you must conceit me,

Either a coward or a flatterer.
That I did love thee, Cæsar, O, 'tis true :
If then thy spirit look upon us now,
Shall it not grieve thee dearer than thy death,
To see thy Antony making his peace,
Shaking the bloody fingers of thy foes,
Most noble ! in the presence of thy corse ?   200
Had I as many eyes as thou hast wounds,
Weeping as fast as they stream forth thy blood,
It would become me better, than to close
In terms of friendship with thine enemies.
Pardon me, Julius !   Here wast thou bay'd, brave hart,
Here didst thou fall, and here thy hunters stand,
Sign'd in thy spoil, and crimson'd in thy lethe.
O world ! thou wast the forest to this hart,
And this, indeed, O world, the heart of thee.
How like a deer, strucken by many princes,   210
Dost thou here lie !

Cas. Mark Antony,—

Ant.   Pardon me, Caius Cassius :
The enemies of Cæsar shall say this ;
Then, in a friend, it is cold modesty.

Cas. I blame you not for praising Cæsar so,
But what compact mean you to have with us ?
Will you be prick'd in number of our friends,

       Or shall we on, and not depend on you ?

Ant. Therefore I took your hands, but was indeed
       Sway'd from the point, by looking down on Cæsar.   220
       Friends am I with you all, and love you all,
       Upon this hope, that you shall give me reasons
       Why, and wherein, Cæsar was dangerous.

Bru. Or else were this a savage spectacle :
       Our reasons are so full of good regard,
       That were you, Antony, the son of Cæsar,
       You should be satisfied.

Ant.   That 's all I seek,
       And am moreover suitor, that I may
       Produce his body to the market-place,
       And in the pulpit, as becomes a friend,   230
       Speak in the order of his funeral.

Bru. You shall, Mark Antony.

Cas.   Brutus, a word with you :
       (aside to Brutus) You know not what you do, do not
          consent
       That Antony speak in his funeral :
       Know you how much the people may be mov'd
       By that which he will utter.

Bru.   By your pardon :
       I will myself into the pulpit first,
       And show the reason of our Cæsar's death.

What Antony shall speak, I will protest   †
He speaks by leave, and by permission ;   240
And that we are contented Cæsar shall
Have all true rites, and lawful ceremonies,
It shall advantage more than do us wrong.

Cas. I know not what may fall, I like it not.

Bru. Mark Antony, here take you Cæsar's body :
    You shall not in your funeral speech blame us,
    But speak all good you can devise of Cæsar,
    And say you do't by our permission ;
    Else shall you not have any hand at all
    About his funeral.   And you shall speak   250
    In the same pulpit whereto I am going,
    After my speech is ended.

Ant.   Be it so;
    I do desire no more.

Bru. Prepare the body then, and follow us.

                        Exeunt all but Antony

Ant. O pardon me, thou bleeding piece of earth,
    That I am meek and gentle with these butchers !
    Thou art the ruins of the noblest man
    That ever lived in the tide of times.
    Woe to the hand that shed this costly blood !
    Over thy wounds, now do I prophesy,   260
    (Which like dumb mouths do ope their ruby lips

To beg the voice and utterance of my tongue)
A curse shall light upon the limbs of men;
Domestic fury, and fierce civil strife,
Shall cumber all the parts of Italy;
Blood and destruction shall be so in use,
And dreadful objects so familiar,
That mothers shall but smile, when they behold
Their infants quarter'd with the hands of war;
All pity chok'd with custom of fell deeds,   270
And Cæsar's spirit ranging for revenge,
With Ate by his side, come hot from hell,
Shall in these confines, with a monarch's voice,
Cry ' Havoc,' and let slip the dogs of war,
That this foul deed shall smell above the earth
With carrion men, groaning for burial.

Enter a Servant

You serve Octavius Cæsar, do you not?

Ser. I do, Mark Antony.

Ant. Cæsar did write for him to come to Rome.

Ser. He did receive his letters, and is coming,   280
And bid me say to you by word of mouth—
O Cæsar!   *Seeing the body*

Ant. Thy heart is big; get thee apart and weep:
Passion, I see, is catching, for mine eyes,
Seeing those beads of sorrow stand in thine,

Began to water.   Is thy master coming ?

Ser. He lies to-night within seven leagues of Rome.

Ant. Post back with speed, and tell him what hath chanc'd :
Here is a mourning Rome, a dangerous Rome,
No Rome of safety for Octavius yet,   290
Hie hence, and tell him so.   Yet stay awhile,
Thou shalt not back, till I have borne this corse
Into the market-place : there shall I try,
In my oration, how the people take
The cruel issue of these bloody men,
According to the which, thou shalt discourse
To young Octavius, of the state of things.
Lend me your hand.   *Exeunt with Cæsar's body*

SCENE II

The Forum

Enter Brutus and Cassius, and a throng of Citizens

Citizens. We will be satisfied ; let us be satisfied.

Bru. Then follow me, and give me audience, friends.
Cassius, go you into the other street,
And part the numbers.
Those that will hear me speak, let 'em stay here ;
Those that will follow Cassius, go with him,

And public reasons shall be rendered
Of Cæsar's death.

1.C.   I will hear Brutus speak.

2.C. I will hear Cassius, and compare their reasons,
When severally we hear them rendered.   10

> *Exit Cassius, with some of the Citizens*
> *Brutus goes into the pulpit*

3.C. The noble Brutus is ascended : silence !

Bru. Be patient till the last.

Romans, countrymen, and lovers, hear me for my †
cause, and be silent, that you may hear. Believe
me for mine honour, and have respect to mine
honour, that you may believe. Censure me in your
wisdom, and awake your senses, that you may the
better judge. If there be any in this assembly, any
dear friend of Cæsar's, to him I say, that Brutus' love
to Cæsar, was no less than his. If then, that friend   20
demand, why Brutus rose against Cæsar, this is my
answer : not that I lov'd Cæsar less, but that I lov'd
Rome more. Had you rather Cæsar were living, and
die all slaves ; than that Cæsar were dead, to live all
free-men ? As Cæsar lov'd me, I weep for him ;
as he was fortunate, I rejoice at it ; as he was valiant,
I honour him : but, as he was ambitious, I slew
him. There is tears, for his love : joy, for his

fortune: honour, for his valour: and death, for
his ambition.   Who is here so base, that would be   30
a bondman?   If any, speak, for him have I offended.
Who is here so rude, that would not be a Roman?
If any, speak, for him have I offended.   Who is here
so vile, that will not love his country?   If any,
speak, for him have I offended.   I pause for a reply.

All. None, Brutus, none.

Bru. Then none have I offended.   I have done no more
to Cæsar, than you shall do to Brutus.   The question
of his death, is enroll'd in the Capitol: his glory not
extenuated, wherein he was worthy; nor his offences   40
enforc'd, for which he suffered death.

     Enter Antony and others, with Cæsar's body

Here comes his body, mourn'd by Mark Antony,
who though he had no hand in his death, shall
receive the benefit of his dying, a place in the
commonwealth, as which of you shall not?   With
this I depart, that, as I slew my best lover for the
good of Rome, I have the same dagger for myself,
when it shall please my country to need my death.

All. Live, Brutus, live, live!

1.*C.* Bring him with triumph home unto his house.   50

2.*C.* Give him a statue with his ancestors.

3.*C.* Let him be Cæsar.

4.*C.*   Cæsar's better parts
     Shall be crown'd in Brutus.

1.*C.* We 'll bring him to his house, with shouts and
     clamours.

Bru. My countrymen,—

2.*C.*   Peace ! silence ! Brutus speaks.

1.*C.* Peace, ho !

Bru. Good Countryman, let me depart alone,
     And (for my sake) stay here with Antony :
     Do grace to Cæsar's corpse, and grace his speech   60
     Tending to Cæsar's glories, which Mark Antony
     (By our permission) is allow'd to make.
     I do entreat you, not a man depart,
     Save I alone, till Antony have spoke.   *Exit*

1.*C.* Stay, ho ! and let us hear Mark Antony.

3.*C.* Let him go up into the public chair,
     We 'll hear him.   Noble Antony, go up.

Ant. For Brutus' sake, I am beholding to you.

                           Goes into the pulpit

4.*C.* What does he say of Brutus ?

3.*C.*   He says, for Brutus' sake
     He finds himself beholding to us all.   70

4.*C.* 'Twere best he speak no harm of Brutus here.

1.*C.* This Cæsar was a tyrant.

3.*C.*   Nay, that 's certain :

We are blest that Rome is rid of him.
2.*C.* Peace ! let us hear what Antony can say.
Ant. You gentle Romans,—
All.   Peace, ho ! let us hear him.
Ant. Friends, Romans, countrymen, lend me your ears :
 I come to bury Cæsar, not to praise him :
 The evil that men do lives after them,
 The good is oft interred with their bones,
 So let it be with Cæsar.   The noble Brutus   80
 Hath told you Cæsar was ambitious :
 If it were so, it was a grievous fault,
 And grievously hath Cæsar answer'd it.
 Here, under leave of Brutus, and the rest,
 (For Brutus is an honourable man,
 So are they all, all honourable men)
 Come I to speak in Cæsar's funeral.
 He was my friend, faithful and just to me ;
 But Brutus says he was ambitious,
 And Brutus is an honourable man.   90
 He hath brought many captives home to Rome,
 Whose ransoms did the general coffers fill :
 Did this in Cæsar seem ambitious ?
 When that the poor have cried, Cæsar hath wept :
 Ambition should be made of sterner stuff,
 Yet Brutus says he was ambitious ;

And Brutus is an honourable man.
You all did see, that on the Lupercal
I thrice presented him a kingly crown,
Which he did thrice refuse. Was this ambition?   100
Yet Brutus says he was ambitious;
And sure he is an honourable man.
I speak not to disprove what Brutus spoke,
But here I am, to speak what I do know;
You all did love him once, not without cause,
What cause withholds you then to mourn for him?
O judgement! thou art fled to brutish beasts,
And men have lost their reason. Bear with me,
My heart is in the coffin there with Cæsar,
And I must pause, till it come back to me.   110

1.*C.* Methinks there is much reason in his sayings.

2.*C.* If thou consider rightly of the matter,
Cæsar has had great wrong.

3.*C.*   Has he, masters?
I fear there will a worse come in his place.

4.*C.* Mark'd ye his words? He would not take the
crown,
Therefore 'tis certain, he was not ambitious.

1.*C.* If it be found so, some will dear abide it,

2.*C.* Poor soul, his eyes are red as fire with weeping.

3.*C.* There's not a nobler man in Rome than Antony.

4.C. Now mark him, he begins again to speak.   120
Ant. But yesterday, the word of Cæsar might
  Have stood against the world : now lies he there,
  And none so poor to do him reverence.
  O masters ! if I were dispos'd to stir
  Your hearts and minds to mutiny and rage,
  I should do Brutus wrong, and Cassius wrong :
  Who (you all know) are honourable men.
  I will not do them wrong : I rather choose
  To wrong the dead, to wrong myself and you,
  Than I will wrong such honourable men.   130
  But here's a parchment, with the seal of Cæsar,
  I found it in his closet, 'tis his will :
  Let but the commons hear this testament
  (Which, pardon me, I do not mean to read)
  And they would go and kiss dead Cæsar's wounds,
  And dip their napkins in his sacred blood ;
  Yea, beg a hair of him for memory,
  And, dying, mention it within their wills,
  Bequeathing it as a rich legacy
  Unto their issue.   140
4.C. We'll hear the will, read it, Mark Antony.
All. The will, the will ! we will hear Cæsar's will.
Ant. Have patience, gentle friends, I must not read it.
  It is not meet you know how Cæsar lov'd you :

You are not wood, you are not stones, but men :
And, being men, hearing the will of Cæsar,
It will inflame you, it will make you mad :
'Tis good you know not that you are his heirs,
For if you should, O, what would come of it ?

4.C. Read the will, we 'll hear it, Antony :   150
You shall read us the will, Cæsar's will.

Ant. Will you be patient ? will you stay awhile ?
I have o'ershot myself to tell you of it,
I fear I wrong the honourable men,
Whose daggers have stabb'd Cæsar ; I do fear it.

4.C. They were traitors : honourable men ?

All. The will ! the testament !

2.C. They were villains, murderers : the will, read the will.

Ant. You will compel me then to read the will :
Then make a ring about the corpse of Cæsar,   160
And let me show you him that made the will :
Shall I descend ? and will you give me leave ?

All. Come down.

2.C. Descend.   *He comes down from the pulpit*

3.C. You shall have leave.

4.C. A ring, stand round.

1.C. Stand from the hearse, stand from the body.

2.C. Room for Antony, most noble Antony.

Ant. Nay, press not so upon me, stand far off.

All. Stand back : room, bear back.   170
Ant. If you have tears, prepare to shed them now.
    You all do know this mantle ; I remember
    The first time ever Cæsar put it on,
    'Twas on a summer's evening in his tent,
    That day he overcame the Nervii :
    Look, in this place ran Cassius' dagger through :
    See what a rent the envious Casca made :
    Through this, the well-beloved Brutus stabb'd,
    And as he pluck'd his cursed steel away,
    Mark how the blood of Cæsar follow'd it,   180
    As rushing out of doors, to be resolv'd
    If Brutus so unkindly knock'd, or no :
    For Brutus, as you know, was Cæsar's angel.
    Judge, O you gods, how dearly Cæsar lov'd him :
    This was the most unkindest cut of all.
    For when the noble Cæsar saw him stab,
    Ingratitude, more strong than traitors' arms,
    Quite vanquish'd him : then burst his mighty heart,
    And in his mantle muffling up his face,
    Even at the base of Pompey's statuë   190
    (Which all the while ran blood) great Cæsar fell.
    O what a fall was there, my countrymen !
    Then I, and you, and all of us fell down,
    Whilst bloody treason flourish'd over us.

71

O now you weep, and I perceive you feel
The dint of pity : these are gracious drops.
Kind souls, what weep you, when you but behold
Our Cæsar's vesture wounded ? Look you here,
Here is himself, marr'd as you see with traitors.

1.C. O piteous spectacle !   200

2.C. O noble Cæsar !

3.C. O woful day !

4.C. O traitors, villains !

1.C. O most bloody sight !

2.C. We will be reveng'd.

All. Revenge ! About ! Seek ! Burn ! Fire ! Kill !
Slay ! Let not a traitor live !

Ant. Stay, countrymen.

1.C. Peace there ! hear the noble Antony.

2.C. We'll hear him, we'll follow him, we'll die with 210
him.

Ant. Good friends, sweet friends, let me not stir you up
To such a sudden flood of mutiny :
They that have done this deed are honourable ;
What private griefs they have, alas, I know not,
That made them do it : they are wise and honourable,
And will, no doubt, with reasons answer you.
I come not, friends, to steal away your hearts,
I am no orator, as Brutus is ;

72

But (as you know me all) a plain blunt man   220
That love my friend, and that they know full well,
That gave me public leave to speak of him :
For I have neither wit, nor words, nor worth,
Action, nor utterance, nor the power of speech,
To stir men's blood : I only speak right on ;
I tell you that which you yourselves do know,
Show you sweet Cæsar's wounds, poor poor dumb
    mouths,
And bid them speak for me : but were I Brutus,
And Brutus Antony, there were an Antony
Would ruffle up your spirits, and put a tongue   230
In every wound of Cæsar, that should move
The stones of Rome to rise and mutiny.

All. We 'll mutiny.

1.C. We 'll burn the house of Brutus.

3.C. Away then, come, seek the conspirators.

Ant. Yet hear me, countrymen, yet hear me speak.

All. Peace, ho !   Hear Antony, most noble Antony !

Ant. Why, friends, you go to do you know not what :
Wherein hath Cæsar thus deserv'd your loves ?
Alas, you know not, I must tell you then :   240
You have forgot the will I told you of.

All. Most true, the will, let 's stay and hear the will.

Ant. Here is the will, and under Cæsar's seal :

To every Roman citizen he gives,
To every several man, seventy-five drachmas.

2.C. Most noble Cæsar, we'll revenge his death.

3.C. O royal Cæsar!

Ant. Hear me with patience.

All. Peace, ho!

Ant. Moreover, he hath left you all his walks,   250
His private arbours, and new-planted orchards,
On this side Tiber, he hath left them you,
And to your heirs for ever; common pleasures,
To walk abroad, and recreate yourselves.
Here was a Cæsar! when comes such another?

1.C. Never, never. Come, away, away!
We'll burn his body in the holy place,
And with the brands fire the traitors' houses.
Take up the body.

2.C. Go fetch fire.   260

3.C. Pluck down benches.

4.C. Pluck down forms, windows, any thing.

                    Exeunt Citizens with the body

Ant. Now let it work: mischief, thou art afoot,
Take thou what course thou wilt.

                Enter a Servant

                      How now, fellow?

Ser. Sir, Octavius is already come to Rome.

Ant. Where is he ?

Ser. He and Lepidus are at Cæsar's house.

Ant. And thither will I straight, to visit him :
  He comes upon a wish.   Fortune is merry,
  And in this mood will give us any thing.   270

Ser. I heard him say, Brutus and Cassius
  Are rid like madmen through the gates of Rome.

Ant. Belike they had some notice of the people,
  How I had mov'd them.   Bring me to Octavius.

                                    Exeunt

                    SCENE III

                    A street

                Enter Cinna the poet

Cin. I dreamt to-night that I did feast with Cæsar,
  And things unluckily charge my fantasy :
  I have no will to wander forth of doors,
  Yet something leads me forth.

                Enter Citizens

1.*C.* What is your name ?

2.*C.* Whither are you going ?

3.*C.* Where do you dwell ?

4.*C.* Are you a married man, or a bachelor ?

2.*C.* Answer every man directly.

                    75

1.C. Ay, and briefly. 10

4.C. Ay, and wisely.

3.C. Ay, and truly, you were best.

Cin. What is my name? Whither am I going? Where
do I dwell? Am I a married man, or a bachelor?
Then, to answer every man, directly and briefly,
wisely and truly: wisely I say, I am a bachelor.

2.C. That's as much as to say, they are fools that marry:
you'll bear me a bang for that, I fear. Proceed;
directly.

Cin. Directly, I am going to Cæsar's funeral. 20

1.C. As a friend or an enemy?

Cin. As a friend.

2.C. That matter is answered directly.

4.C. For your dwelling; briefly.

Cin. Briefly, I dwell by the Capitol.

3.C. Your name, sir, truly.

Cin. Truly, my name is Cinna.

1.C. Tear him to pieces, he's a conspirator.

Cin. I am Cinna the poet, I am Cinna the poet.

4.C. Tear him for his bad verses, tear him for his bad 30
verses.

Cin. I am not Cinna the conspirator.

4.C. It is no matter, his name's Cinna, pluck but his
name out of his heart, and turn him going.

3.C. Tear him, tear him ! Come, brands, ho, fire-brands !
  to Brutus', to Cassius', burn all. Some to Decius'
  house, and some to Casca's ; some to Ligarius' :
  away, go !   *Exeunt*

Act Fourth

SCENE I

A house in Rome

Antony, Octavius, and Lepidus, seated at a table

Ant. These many then shall die ; their names are prick'd.
Oct. Your brother too must die ; consent you, Lepidus ?
Lep. I do consent—
Oct.   Prick him down, Antony.
Lep. Upon condition Publius shall not live,
  Who is your sister's son, Mark Antony,
Ant. He shall not live ; look, with a spot I damn him.
  But, Lepidus, go you to Cæsar's house :
  Fetch the will hither, and we shall determine
  How to cut off some charge in legacies.
Lep. What, shall I find you here ?   10
Oct. Or here, or at the Capitol.   *Exit Lepidus*
Ant. This is a slight unmeritable man,

77

Meet to be sent on errands : is it fit,
The three-fold world divided, he should stand
One of the three to share it ?

Oct. So you thought him,
And took his voice who should be prick'd to die
In our black sentence and proscription.

Ant. Octavius, I have seen more days than you,
And though we lay these honours on this man,
To ease ourselves of divers slanderous loads, 20
He shall but bear them as the ass bears gold,
To groan and sweat under the business,
Either led or driven, as we point the way :
And having brought our treasure where we will,
Then take we down his load, and turn him off
(Like to the empty ass) to shake his ears,
And graze in commons.

Oct. You may do your will :
But he 's a tried and valiant soldier.

Ant. So is my horse, Octavius, and for that
I do appoint him store of provender : 30
It is a creature that I teach to fight,
To wind, to stop, to run directly on,
His corporal motion govern'd by my spirit ;
And, in some taste, is Lepidus but so ;
He must be taught, and train'd, and bid go forth ;

A barren-spirited fellow ; one that feeds
On objects, arts and imitations,   †
Which, out of use, and stal'd by other men,
Begin his fashion.   Do not talk of him,
But as a property.   And now, Octavius,   40
Listen great things.   Brutus and Cassius
Are levying powers ; we must straight make head :
Therefore let our alliance be combin'd,
Our best friends made, our means stretch'd,
And let us presently go sit in council,
How covert matters may be best disclos'd,
And open perils surest answered.

Oct. Let us do so : for we are at the stake,
And bay'd about with many enemies,
And some that smile have in their hearts, I fear,   50
Millions of mischiefs.   *Exeunt*

SCENES II AND III

Camp near Sardis.   Before Brutus's tent

*Drum.   Enter Brutus, Lucilius, Lucius, and Soldiers ;
Titinius and Pindarus meet them*

Bru. Stand, ho !
Lucil. Give the word, ho ! and stand.

Bru. What now, Lucilius ? is Cassius near ?

Lucil. He is at hand, and Pindarus is come
    To do you salutation from his master.

Bru. He greets me well.   Your master, Pindarus,
    In his own change, or by ill officers,
    Hath given me some worthy cause to wish
    Things done, undone : but if he be at hand,
    I shall be satisfied.

Pin.   I do not doubt   10
    But that my noble master will appear
    Such as he is, full of regard and honour.

Bru. He is not doubted.   A word, Lucilius,
    How he receiv'd you : let me be resolv'd.

Lucil. With courtesy, and with respect enough,
    But not with such familiar instances,
    Nor with such free and friendly conference,
    As he hath us'd of old.

Bru.   Thou hast describ'd
    A hot friend, cooling : ever note, Lucilius,
    When love begins to sicken and decay,   20
    It useth an enforced ceremony.
    There are no tricks in plain and simple faith :
    But hollow men, like horses hot at hand,
    Make gallant show, and promise of their mettle ;
    But when they should endure the bloody spur,

They fall their crests, and like deceitful jades
Sink in the trial.   Comes his army on ?

Lucil. They mean this night in Sardis to be quarter'd ;
The greater part, the horse in general,
Are come with Cassius.   *Low march within*

Bru.   Hark, he is arrived :   30
March gently on to meet him.

                    Enter Cassius and his powers

Cas. Stand, ho !

Bru. Stand, ho !   Speak the word along.

1.S. Stand !

2.S. Stand !

3.S. Stand !

Cas. Most noble brother, you have done me wrong.

Bru. Judge me, you gods ! wrong I mine enemies ?
And if not so, how should I wrong a brother ?

Cas. Brutus, this sober form of yours hides wrongs,   40
And when you do them—

Bru.   Cassius, be content,
Speak your griefs softly, I do know you well.
Before the eyes of both our armies here
(Which should perceive nothing but love from us)
Let us not wrangle.   Bid them move away ;
Then in my tent, Cassius, enlarge your griefs,
And I will give you audience.

81

Cas.   Pindarus,
    Bid our commanders lead their charges off
    A little from this ground.
Bru. Lucilius, do you the like, and let no man   †
    Come to our tent, till we have done our conference.   51
    Let Lucius and Titinius guard our door.

              Exeunt all but Brutus and Cassius,
                who enter the tent   †

Cas. That you have wrong'd me, doth appear in this :
    You have condemn'd and noted Lucius Pella
    For taking bribes here of the Sardians ;
    Wherein my letters, praying on his side,
    Because I knew the man, was slighted off.
Bru. You wrong'd yourself to write in such a case.
Cas. In such a time as this, it is not meet
    That every nice offence should bear his comment.
Bru. Let me tell you, Cassius, you yourself
    Are much condemn'd to have an itching palm,   10
    To sell and mart your offices for gold
    To undeservers.
Cas.   I, an itching palm ?

You know that you are Brutus that speaks this,
Or, by the gods, this speech were else your last.

Bru. The name of Cassius honours this corruption,
And chastisement doth therefore hide his head.

Cas. Chastisement?

Bru. Remember March, the ides of March remember:
Did not great Julius bleed for justice' sake?
What villain touch'd his body, that did stab,   20
And not for justice?   What? shall one of us,
That struck the foremost man of all this world
But for supporting robbers, shall we now
Contaminate our fingers, with base bribes?
And sell the mighty space of our large honours
For so much trash as may be grasped thus?
I had rather be a dog, and bay the moon,
Than such a Roman.

Cas.   Brutus, bait not me,
I 'll not endure it: you forget yourself
To hedge me in; I am a soldier, I,   30
Older in practice, abler than yourself
To make conditions.

Bru.   Go to; you are not, Cassius.

Cas. I am.

Bru. I say, you are not.

Cas. Urge me no more, I shall forget myself;

Have mind upon your health ; tempt me no farther.

Bru. Away, slight man !

Cas. Is 't possible ?

Bru.   Hear me, for I will speak.
Must I give way and room to your rash choler ?
Shall I be frighted, when a madman stares ?   40

Cas. O ye gods, ye gods ! must I endure all this ?

Bru. All this ? ay, more : fret till your proud heart break.
Go show your slaves how choleric you are,
And make your bondmen tremble.   Must I budge ?
Must I observe you ? must I stand and crouch
Under your testy humour ? By the gods,
You shall digest the venom of your spleen
Though it do split you. For, from this day forth,
I 'll use you for my mirth, yea, for my laughter,
When you are waspish.

Cas.   Is it come to this ?   50

Bru. You say, you are a better soldier :
Let it appear so ; make your vaunting true,
And it shall please me well. For mine own part,
I shall be glad to learn of noble men.

Cas. You wrong me every way ; you wrong me, Brutus ;
I said, an elder soldier, not a better :
Did I say, better ?

Bru.   If you did, I care not.

Cas. When Cæsar liv'd, he durst not thus have mov'd me.

Bru. Peace, peace ! you durst not so have tempted him.

Cas. I durst not ?   60

Bru. No.

Cas. What ? durst not tempt him ?

Bru.   For your life you durst not.

Cas. Do not presume too much upon my love,
    I may do that I shall be sorry for.

Bru. You have done that you should be sorry for.
    There is no terror, Cassius, in your threats ;
    For I am arm'd so strong in honesty,
    That they pass by me, as the idle wind,
    Which I respect not.   I did send to you
    For certain sums of gold, which you denied me,   70
    For I can raise no money by vile means :
    By heaven, I had rather coin my heart,
    And drop my blood for drachmas, than to wring
    From the hard hands of peasants their vile trash
    By any indirection.   I did send
    To you for gold to pay my legions,
    Which you denied me : was that done like Cassius ?
    Should I have answer'd Caius Cassius so ?
    When Marcus Brutus grows so covetous,
    To lock such rascal counters from his friends,   80
    Be ready, gods, with all your thunderbolts,

    Dash him to pieces!

Cas.   I denied you not.

Bru. You did.

Cas.   I did not. He was but a fool
    That brought my answer back. Brutus hath riv'd
        my heart:
    A friend should bear his friend's infirmities;
    But Brutus makes mine greater than they are.

Bru. I do not, till you practise them on me.

Cas. You love me not.

Bru.   I do not like your faults.

Cas. A friendly eye could never see such faults.

Bru. A flatterer's would not, though they do appear   90
    As huge as high Olympus.

Cas. Come, Antony, and young Octavius, come,
    Revenge yourselves alone on Cassius,
    For Cassius is aweary of the world;
    Hated by one he loves, brav'd by his brother,
    Check'd like a bondman, all his faults observ'd,
    Set in a note-book, learn'd, and conn'd by rote,
    To cast into my teeth. O, I could weep
    My spirit from mine eyes! There is my dagger,
    And here my naked breast; within, a heart   100
    Dearer than Plutus' mine, richer than gold:
    If that thou be'st a Roman, take it forth;

I, that denied thee gold, will give my heart :
Strike, as thou didst at Cæsar ; for I know,
When thou didst hate him worst, thou lovedst him
    better
Than ever thou lovedst Cassius.

Bru.   Sheathe your dagger :
Be angry when you will, it shall have scope ;
Do what you will, dishonour shall be humour.
O Cassius, you are yoked with a lamb,
That carries anger as the flint bears fire,   110
Who, much enforced, shows a hasty spark,
And straight is cold again.

Cas.   Hath Cassius liv'd
To be but mirth and laughter to his Brutus,
When grief and blood ill-temper'd vexeth him.

Bru. When I spoke that, I was ill-temper'd too.

Cas. Do you confess so much ?   Give me your hand.

Bru. And my heart too.

Cas.   O Brutus !

Bru.   What 's the matter ?

Cas. Have not you love enough to bear with me,
When that rash humour which my mother gave me
Makes me forgetful ?

Bru.   Yes, Cassius, and from henceforth, 120
When you are over-earnest with your Brutus,

He'll think your mother chides, and leave you so.

Poet. (*within*) Let me go in to see the generals;
There is some grudge between 'em, 'tis not meet
They be alone.

Luc. (*within*) You shall not come to them.

Poet. (*within*) Nothing but death shall stay me.

Enter Poet, followed by Lucilius, Titinius, and Lucius

Cas. How now? what's the matter?

Poet. For shame, you generals! what do you mean?
Love, and be friends, as two such men should be,   130
For I have seen more years, I'm sure, than ye.

Cas. Ha, ha! how vilely doth this cynic rhyme!

Bru. Get you hence, sirrah; saucy fellow, hence!

Cas. Bear with him, Brutus, 'tis his fashion.

Bru. I'll know his humour, when he knows his time:
What should the wars do with these jigging fools?
Companion, hence!

Cas.   Away, away, be gone!   *Exit Poet*

Bru. Lucilius and Titinius, bid the commanders
Prepare to lodge their companies to-night.

Cas. And come yourselves, and bring Messala with you   140
Immediately to us.   *Exeunt Lucilius and Titinius*

Bru.   Lucius, a bowl of wine!   *Exit Lucius*

Cas. I did not think you could have been so angry.

Bru. O Cassius, I am sick of many griefs.

Cas. Of your philosophy you make no use,
    If you give place to accidental evils.

Bru. No man bears sorrow better.   Portia is dead.

Cas. Ha ? Portia ?

Bru. She is dead.

Cas. How 'scap'd I killing, when I cross'd you so ?
    O insupportable and touching loss !   150
    Upon what sickness ?

Bru.   Impatient of my absence,
    And grief, that young Octavius with Mark Antony
    Have made themselves so strong : for with her death
    That tidings came.   With this she fell distract,
    And (her attendants absent) swallow'd fire.   †

Cas. And died so ?

Bru.   Even so.

Cas.   O ye immortal gods !

Re-enter Lucius, with wine and taper

Bru. Speak no more of her : give me a bowl of wine,
    In this I bury all unkindness, Cassius.   *Drinks*

Cas. My heart is thirsty for that noble pledge.
    Fill, Lucius, till the wine o'erswell the cup ;   160
    I cannot drink too much of Brutus' love.   *Drinks*

Bru. Come in, Titinius !

    Re-enter Titinius, with Messala
        Welcome, good Messala.

Now sit we close about this taper here,
And call in question our necessities.

Cas. Portia, art thou gone?

Bru.   No more, I pray you.
Messala, I have here received letters,
That young Octavius, and Mark Antony,
Come down upon us with a mighty power,
Bending their expedition toward Philippi.

Mes. Myself have letters of the self-same tenour.   170

Bru. With what addition?

Mes. That by proscription, and bills of outlawry,
Octavius, Antony, and Lepidus,
Have put to death an hundred senators.

Bru. Therein our letters do not well agree;
Mine speak of seventy senators that died
By their proscriptions, Cicero being one.

Cas. Cicero one?

Mes.   Cicero is dead,
And by that order of proscription.
Had you your letters from your wife, my lord?   180

Bru. No, Messala.

Mes. Nor nothing in your letters writ of her?

Bru. Nothing, Messala.   †

Mes.   That, methinks, is strange.

Bru. Why ask you? hear you aught of her, in yours?

Mes. No, my lord.

Bru. Now, as you are a Roman, tell me true.

Mes. Then like a Roman bear the truth I tell :
  For certain she is dead, and by strange manner.

Bru. Why, farewell, Portia.   We must die, Messala :
  With meditating that she must die once,   190
  I have the patience to endure it now.

Mes. Even so great men great losses should endure.

Cas. I have as much of this in art as you,
  But yet my nature could not bear it so.

Bru. Well, to our work alive.   What do you think
  Of marching to Philippi presently ?

Cas. I do not think it good.

Bru.   Your reason ?

Cas.   This it is :
  'Tis better that the enemy seek us,
  So shall he waste his means, weary his soldiers,
  Doing himself offence, whilst we, lying still,   200
  Are full of rest, defence, and nimbleness.

Bru. Good reasons must of force give place to better :
  The people 'twixt Philippi and this ground
  Do stand but in a forc'd affection ;
  For they have grudg'd us contribution :
  The enemy, marching along by them,
  By them shall make a fuller number up,

Come on refresh'd, new-added, and encourag'd ;
From which advantage shall we cut him off,
If at Philippi we do face him there,   210
These people at our back.

Cas.   Hear me, good brother.

Bru. Under your pardon.   You must note beside,
That we have tried the utmost of our friends ;
Our legions are brim-full, our cause is ripe,
The enemy increaseth every day,
We, at the height, are ready to decline.
There is a tide in the affairs of men,
Which taken at the flood leads on to fortune ;
Omitted, all the voyage of their life
Is bound in shallows and in miseries.   220
On such a full sea are we now afloat,
And we must take the current when it serves,
Or lose our ventures.

Cas.   Then, with your will, go on ;
We 'll along ourselves, and meet them at Philippi.

Bru. The deep of night is crept upon our talk,
And nature must obey necessity,
Which we will niggard with a little rest.
There is no more to say.

Cas.   No more ; good night ;
Early to-morrow will we rise, and hence.

Bru. Lucius, my gown.   Farewell, good Messala,   230
  Good night, Titinius : noble, noble Cassius,
  Good night, and good repose.

Cas.   O my dear brother !
  This was an ill beginning of the night :
  Never come such division 'tween our souls !
  Let it not, Brutus.

Bru.   Every thing is well.

Cas. Good night, my lord.

Bru.   Good night, good brother.

Tit. Mes. Good night, Lord Brutus.

Bru.   Farewell, every one.

        Exeunt all but Brutus

   Re-enter Lucius, with the gown

  Give me the gown.   Where is thy instrument ?

Luc. Here in the tent.

Bru.   What, thou speak'st drowsily ?
  Poor knave, I blame thee not, thou art o'er-watch'd. 240
  Call Claudius, and some other of my men,
  I 'll have them sleep on cushions in my tent.

Luc. Varro and Claudius !

    Enter Varro and Claudius

Var. Calls my lord ?

Bru. I pray you, sirs, lie in my tent and sleep ;
  It may be I shall raise you by and by

On business to my brother Cassius.

Var. So please you, we will stand, and watch your pleasure.

Bru. I will not have it so : lie down, good sirs,

It may be I shall otherwise bethink me.   250

Look, Lucius, here's the book I sought for so ;

I put it in the pocket of my gown.

Varro and Claudius lie down

Luc. I was sure your lordship did not give it me.

Bru. Bear with me, good boy, I am much forgetful.

Canst thou hold up thy heavy eyes awhile,

And touch thy instrument a strain or two ?

Luc. Ay, my lord, an't please you.

Bru.   It does, my boy :

I trouble thee too much, but thou art willing.

Luc. It is my duty, sir.

Bru. I should not urge thy duty past thy might,   260

I know young bloods look for a time of rest.

Luc. I have slept, my lord, already.

Bru. It was well done, and thou shalt sleep again ;

I will not hold thee long.   If I do live,

I will be good to thee.   *Music, and a song*

This is a sleepy tune : O murderous slumber,

Lay'st thou thy leaden mace upon my boy,

That plays thee music ?   Gentle knave, good night :

I will not do thee so much wrong to wake thee :

If thou dost nod, thou break'st thy instrument,   270
I 'll take it from thee, and, good boy, good night.
Let me see, let me see ; is not the leaf turn'd down
Where I left reading ?   Here it is, I think.

Sits down

Enter the Ghost of Cæsar

How ill this taper burns !   Ha ! who comes here ?
I think it is the weakness of mine eyes
That shapes this monstrous apparition.
It comes upon me : art thou any thing ?
Art thou some god, some angel, or some devil,
That mak'st my blood cold, and my hair to stare ?
Speak to me, what thou art.   280

Gho. Thy evil spirit, Brutus.

Bru.   Why com'st thou ?

Gho. To tell thee thou shalt see me at Philippi.

Bru. Well ; then I shall see thee again ?

Gho. Ay, at Philippi.

Bru. Why, I will see thee at Philippi then.   *Exit Ghost*
Now I have taken heart, thou vanishest.
Ill spirit, I would hold more talk with thee.
Boy, Lucius ! Varro ! Claudius ! Sirs, awake !
Claudius !

Luc. The strings, my lord, are false.   290

Bru. He thinks he still is at his instrument.

Lucius, awake !

Luc. My lord ?

Bru. Didst thou dream, Lucius, that thou so criedst out ?

Luc. My lord, I do not know that I did cry.

Bru. Yes, that thou didst : didst thou see any thing ?

Luc. Nothing, my lord.

Bru. Sleep again, Lucius.   Sirrah Claudius !

    (*to Var.*) Fellow thou, awake !

Var. My lord ?   300

Cla. My lord ?

Bru. Why did you so cry out, sirs, in your sleep ?

Var. Cla. Did we, my lord ?

Bru.   Ay : saw you any thing ?

Var. No, my lord, I saw nothing.

Cla.   Nor I, my lord.

Bru. Go, and commend me to my brother Cassius ;

    Bid him set on his powers betimes before,

    And we will follow.

Var. Cla.   It shall be done, my lord.   *Exeunt*

Act Fifth

SCENE I

The plains of Philippi

Enter Octavius, Antony, and their army

Oct. Now, Antony, our hopes are answered ;
    You said the enemy would not come down,
    But keep the hills and upper regions ;
    It proves not so : their battles are at hand,
    They mean to warn us at Philippi here,
    Answering before we do demand of them.
Ant. Tut, I am in their bosoms, and I know
    Wherefore they do it : they could be content
    To visit other places, and come down
    With fearful bravery ; thinking by this face   10
    To fasten in our thoughts that they have courage ;
    But 'tis not so.

              Enter a Messenger

Mes.   Prepare you, generals,
    The enemy comes on in gallant show ;
    Their bloody sign of battle is hung out,
    And something to be done immediately.

Ant. Octavius, lead your battle softly on
   Upon the left hand of the even field.

Oct. Upon the right hand I, keep thou the left.

Ant. Why do you cross me in this exigent ?

Oct. I do not cross you : but I will do so.   *March* 20

   Drum. Enter Brutus, Cassius, and their Army ;
   Lucilius, Titinius, Messala, and others

Bru. They stand, and would have parley.

Cas. Stand fast, Titinius, we must out and talk.

Oct. Mark Antony, shall we give sign of battle ?

Ant. No, Cæsar, we will answer on their charge.
   Make forth, the generals would have some words.

Oct. Stir not until the signal.

Bru. Words before blows : is it so, countrymen ?

Oct. Not that we love words better, as you do.

Bru. Good words are better than bad strokes, Octavius.

Ant. In your bad strokes, Brutus, you give good words :   30
   Witness the hole you made in Cæsar's heart,
   Crying ' Long live ! hail, Cæsar ! '

Cas.   Antony,
   The posture of your blows are yet unknown ;
   But for your words, they rob the Hybla bees,
   And leave them honeyless.

Ant.   Not stingless too.

Bru. O, yes, and soundless too ;

For you have stol'n their buzzing, Antony,
And very wisely threat before you sting.

Ant. Villains you did not so, when your vile daggers
Hack'd one another in the sides of Cæsar :   40
You show'd your teeth like apes, and fawn'd like
      hounds,
And bow'd like bondmen, kissing Cæsar's feet ;
Whilst damned Casca, like a cur, behind
Struck Cæsar on the neck.   O you flatterers !

Cas. Flatterers ?   Now, Brutus, thank yourself,
This tongue had not offended so to-day,
If Cassius might have rul'd.

Oct. Come, come, the cause.   If arguing make us sweat,
The proof of it will turn to redder drops :
Look,
I draw a sword against conspirators,   50
When think you that the sword goes up again ?
Never, till Cæsar's three and thirty wounds
Be well aveng'd ; or till another Cæsar
Have added slaughter to the sword of traitors.

Bru. Cæsar, thou canst not die by traitors' hands,
Unless thou bring'st them with thee.

Oct.   So I hope ;
I was not born to die on Brutus' sword.

Bru. O, if thou wert the noblest of thy strain,

Young man, thou couldst not die more honourable.

Cas. A peevish schoolboy, worthless of such honour,   60
Join'd with a masquer and a reveller !

Ant. Old Cassius still !

Oct.   Come, Antony ; away !
Defiance, traitors, hurl we in your teeth ;
If you dare fight to-day, come to the field :
If not, when you have stomachs.

              Exeunt Octavius, Antony, and their army

Cas. Why, now, blow wind, swell billow, and swim bark !
The storm is up, and all is on the hazard.

Bru. Ho, Lucilius ! hark, a word with you.

Lucil.   *(standing forth)* My lord ?

            Brutus and Lucilius converse apart

Cas. Messala !

Mes. *(standing forth)* What says my general ?

Cas.   Messala,   70
This is my birth-day ; as this very day
Was Cassius born. Give me thy hand, Messala :
Be thou my witness, that against my will
(As Pompey was) am I compell'd to set
Upon one battle all our liberties.
You know that I held Epicurus strong,
And his opinion : now I change my mind,
And partly credit things that do presage.

Coming from Sardis, on our former ensign
Two mighty eagles fell, and there they perch'd,   80
Gorging and feeding from our soldiers' hands,
Who to Philippi here consorted us :
This morning are they fled away and gone,
And in their steads do ravens, crows, and kites
Fly o'er our heads, and downward look on us,
As we were sickly prey ; their shadows seem
A canopy most fatal, under which
Our army lies, ready to give up the ghost.

Mes. Believe not so.

Cas.   I but believe it partly,
For I am fresh of spirit, and resolv'd   90
To meet all perils very constantly.

Bru. Even so, Lucilius.

Cas.   Now, most noble Brutus,
The gods to-day stand friendly, that we may,
Lovers in peace, lead on our days to age !
But, since the affairs of men rests still incertain,
Let 's reason with the worst that may befall.
If we do lose this battle, then is this
The very last time we shall speak together :
What are you then determined to do ?

Bru. Even by the rule of that philosophy,   100
By which I did blame Cato, for the death

Which he did give himself : I know not how,
But I do find it cowardly and vile,
For fear of what might fall, so to prevent
The time of life, arming myself with patience
To stay the providence of some high powers,
That govern us below.

Cas.   Then, if we lose this battle,
You are contented to be led in triumph
Thorough the streets of Rome ?

Bru. No, Cassius, no : think not, thou noble Roman,   110
That ever Brutus will go bound to Rome ;
He bears too great a mind.   But this same day
Must end that work the ides of March begun.
And whether we shall meet again, I know not :
Therefore our everlasting farewell take :
For ever, and for ever, farewell, Cassius !
If we do meet again, why, we shall smile ;
If not, why then this parting was well made.

Cas. For ever, and for ever, farewell, Brutus !
If we do meet again, we 'll smile indeed ;   120
If not, 'tis true, this parting was well made.

Bru. Why then, lead on.   O, that a man might know
The end of this day's business, ere it come !
But it sufficeth, that the day will end,
And then the end is known.   Come, ho! away!   *Exeunt*

SCENES II–V

Various parts of the field of battle

Alarum.   Enter Brutus and Messala

Bru. Ride, ride, Messala, ride, and give these bills
    Unto the legions, on the other side :   *Loud alarum*
    Let them set on at once ; for I perceive
    But cold demeanour in Octavius' wing ;
    And sudden push gives them the overthrow :   †
    Ride, ride, Messala, let them all come down.

                                          Exeunt

Alarums.   Enter Cassius and Titinius

Cas. O, look, Titinius, look, the villains fly !
    Myself have to mine own turn'd enemy :
    This ensign here of mine was turning back,
    I slew the coward, and did take it from him.

Tit. O Cassius, Brutus gave the word too early,
    Who, having some advantage on Octavius,
    Took it too eagerly : his soldiers fell to spoil,
    Whilst we by Antony are all enclos'd.

Enter Pindarus

Pin. Fly further off, my lord, fly further off;
    Mark Antony is in your tents, my lord: 10
    Fly, therefore, noble Cassius, fly far off.

Cas. This hill is far enough.   Look, look, Titinius,
    Are those my tents where I perceive the fire?

Tit. They are, my lord.

Cas.   Titinius, if thou lovest me,
    Mount thou my horse, and hide thy spurs in him,
    Till he have brought thee up to yonder troops
    And here again, that I may rest assur'd
    Whether yond troops are friend or enemy.

Tit. I will be here again, even with a thought.   *Exit*

Cas. Go, Pindarus, get higher on that hill,   20
    My sight was ever thick: regard Titinius,
    And tell me what thou not'st about the field.

                    Pindarus ascends the hill

    This day I breathed first, time is come round,
    And where I did begin, there shall I end,
    My life is run his compass.   Sirrah, what news?

Pin. (*above*) O my lord!

Cas. What news?

Pin. (*above*) Titinius is enclosed round about
    With horsemen, that make to him on the spur,
    Yet he spurs on.   Now they are almost on him: 30

Now, Titinius ! Now some light : O, he lights too.
He's ta'en. (*Shout.*) And, hark ! they shout for joy.
Cas. Come down, behold no more :
  O, coward that I am, to live so long,
  To see my best friend ta'en before my face !
    Pindarus descends
  Come hither, sirrah :
  In Parthia did I take thee prisoner,
  And then I swore thee, saving of thy life,
  That whatsoever I did bid thee do,
  Thou shouldst attempt it.   Come now, keep thine
  oath,   40
  Now be a free-man, and with this good sword,
  That ran through Cæsar's bowels, search this bosom.
  Stand not to answer : here, take thou the hilts,
  And when my face is cover'd, as 'tis now,
  Guide thou the sword. (*Pindarus stabs him.*) Cæsar,
  thou art reveng'd,
  Even with the sword that kill'd thee. *Dies*
Pin. So, I am free, yet would not so have been,
  Durst I have done my will.   O Cassius !
  Far from this country Pindarus shall run,
  Where never Roman shall take note of him. *Exit* 50
   Re-enter Titinius with Messala
Mes. It is but change, Titinius ; for Octavius

105

      Is overthrown by noble Brutus' power,
      As Cassius' legions are by Antony.
Tit. These tidings will well comfort Cassius.
Mes. Where did you leave him ?
Tit.   All disconsolate,
      With Pindarus his bondman, on this hill.
Mes. Is not that he that lies upon the ground ?
Tit. He lies not like the living.   O my heart !
Mes. Is not that he ?
Tit.   No, this was he, Messala,
      But Cassius is no more.   O setting sun,   60
      As in thy red rays thou dost sink to night,
      So in his red blood Cassius' day is set,
      The sun of Rome is set !   Our day is gone,
      Clouds, dews, and dangers come ; our deeds are done !
      Mistrust of my success hath done this deed.
Mes. Mistrust of good success hath done this deed.
      O hateful error, melancholy's child,
      Why dost thou show to the apt thoughts of men
      The things that are not ?   O error, soon conceiv'd,
      Thou never com'st unto a happy birth,   70
      But kill'st the mother that engender'd thee !
Tit. What, Pindarus ? where art thou, Pindarus ?
Mes. Seek him, Titinius, whilst I go to meet
      The noble Brutus, thrusting this report

Into his ears : I may say ' thrusting ' it ;
For piercing steel, and darts envenomed,
Shall be as welcome to the ears of Brutus
As tidings of this sight.

Tit.   Hie you, Messala,
And I will seek for Pindarus the while.   *Exit Messala*
Why didst thou send me forth, brave Cassius ?   80
Did I not meet thy friends, and did not they
Put on my brows this wreath of victory,
And bid me give it thee ?   Didst thou not hear their
    shouts ?
Alas, thou hast misconstrued every thing !
But, hold thee, take this garland on thy brow,
Thy Brutus bid me give it thee, and I
Will do his bidding.   Brutus, come apace,
And see how I regarded Caius Cassius.
By your leave, gods : this is a Roman's part :
Come, Cassius' sword, and find Titinius' heart.   90

Kills himself

*Alarum.   Re-enter Messala, with Brutus, young Cato,
Strato, Volumnius, and Lucilius*

Bru. Where, where, Messala, doth his body lie ?
Mes. Lo, yonder, and Titinius mourning it.
Bru. Titinius' face is upward.
Cat.   He is slain.

107

Bru. O Julius Cæsar, thou art mighty yet,
    Thy spirit walks abroad, and turns our swords
    In our own proper entrails.   *Low alarums* †
Cat.   Brave Titinius !
    Look, whe'er he have not crown'd dead Cassius !
Bru. Are yet two Romans living such as these ?
    The last of all the Romans, fare thee well !
    It is impossible that ever Rome   100
    Should breed thy fellow.   Friends, I owe moe tears
    To this dead man than you shall see me pay.
    I shall find time, Cassius : I shall find time.
    Come therefore, and to Thasos send his body,
    His funerals shall not be in our camp,
    Lest it discomfort us.   Lucilius, come,
    And come, young Cato, let us to the field :
    Labeo and Flavius, set our battles on.
    'Tis three o'clock, and, Romans, yet ere night
    We shall try fortune in a second fight.   *Exeunt* 110

      Alarum.   *Enter Brutus, Messala, young Cato, Lucilius,*
                  and Flavius

Bru. Yet, countrymen, O, yet hold up your heads !
Cat. What bastard doth not ?   Who will go with me ?

I will proclaim my name about the field.
I am the son of Marcus Cato, ho !
A foe to tyrants, and my country's friend.
I am the son of Marcus Cato, ho !

Enter soldiers, and fight

Bru. And I am Brutus, Marcus Brutus, I ;
Brutus, my country's friend ; know me for Brutus !

Exit

Lucil. O young and noble Cato, art thou down ?
Why, now thou diest as bravely as Titinius,   10
And mayst be honour'd, being Cato's son.

First Sold. Yield, or thou diest.

Lucil.   Only I yield to die :
(*offering money*) There is so much, that thou wilt kill
          me straight ;
Kill Brutus, and be honour'd in his death.

First Sold. We must not : a noble prisoner !

Sec. Sold. Room, ho !   Tell Antony, Brutus is ta'en.

First Sold. I 'll tell the news.   Here comes the general.

Enter Antony

Brutus is ta'en, Brutus is ta'en, my lord.

Ant. Where is he ?

Lucil. Safe, Antony, Brutus is safe enough :   20
I dare assure thee, that no enemy
Shall ever take alive the noble Brutus :

The gods defend him from so great a shame !
When you do find him, or alive, or dead,
He will be found like Brutus, like himself.

Ant. This is not Brutus, friend, but, I assure you,
A prize no less in worth ; keep this man safe,
Give him all kindness.   I had rather have
Such men my friends than enemies.   Go on,
And see whe'er Brutus be alive or dead,   30
And bring us word, unto Octavius' tent,
How every thing is chanc'd.   *Exeunt*

Enter Brutus, Dardanius, Clitus, Strato, and Volumnius

Bru. Come, poor remains of friends, rest on this rock.
Cli. Statilius show'd the torch-light, but, my lord,
He came not back : he is or ta'en or slain.
Bru. Sit thee down, Clitus ; slaying is the word,
It is a deed in fashion.   Hark thee, Clitus.
                                              Whispering
Cli. What, I, my lord ?   No, not for all the world.
Bru. Peace then, no words.
Cli.   I 'll rather kill myself.
Bru. Hark thee, Dardanius.   *Whispering*

Dar.   Shall I do such a deed ?

Cli. O Dardanius !

Dar. O Clitus !   10

Cli. What ill request did Brutus make to thee ?

Dar. To kill him, Clitus : look, he meditates.

Cli. Now is that noble vessel full of grief,
　　That it runs over even at his eyes.

Bru. Come hither, good Volumnius, list a word.

Vol. What says my lord ?

Bru.   Why, this, Volumnius :
　　The ghost of Cæsar hath appear'd to me
　　Two several times by night ; at Sardis, once ;
　　And this last night, here in Philippi fields :
　　I know my hour is come.

Vol.   Not so, my lord.   20

Bru. Nay, I am sure it is, Volumnius.
　　Thou seest the world, Volumnius, how it goes,
　　Our enemies have beat us to the pit :   *Low alarums*
　　It is more worthy, to leap in ourselves,
　　Than tarry till they push us.   Good Volumnius,
　　Thou know'st that we two went to school together :
　　Even for that our love of old, I prithee
　　Hold thou my sword-hilts, whilst I run on it.

Vol. That's not an office for a friend, my lord.

                              Alarum still

III

Cli. Fly, fly, my lord, there is no tarrying here.　　　　30

Bru. Farewell to you, and you, and you, Volumnius.
　　　Strato, thou hast been all this while asleep ;
　　　Farewell to thee too, Strato.　Countrymen,
　　　My heart doth joy, that yet in all my life
　　　I found no man but he was true to me.
　　　I shall have glory by this losing day
　　　More than Octavius, and Mark Antony,
　　　By this vile conquest shall attain unto.
　　　So, fare you well at once, for Brutus' tongue
　　　Hath almost ended his life's history :　　　　40
　　　Night hangs upon mine eyes, my bones would rest,
　　　That have but labour'd to attain this hour.

　　　　　　　Alarum.　Cry within, ' Fly, fly, fly !'

Cli. Fly, my lord, fly.

Bru.　　　　　　Hence ! I will follow.

　　　　　　　Exeunt Clitus, Dardanius, and Volumnius

　　　I prithee, Strato, stay thou by thy lord,
　　　Thou art a fellow of a good respect ;
　　　Thy life hath had some smatch of honour in it,
　　　Hold then my sword, and turn away thy face,
　　　While I do run upon it.　Wilt thou, Strato ?

Str. Give me your hand first.　Fare you well, my lord.

Bru. Farewell, good Strato.　(*Runs on his sword.*)　Cæsar,
　　　now be still,　　　　50

112

I kill'd not thee with half so good a will.   *Dies*
  Alarum.   Retreat.   Enter Octavius, Antony, Messala,
                Lucilius, and the army

Oct. What man is that?

Mes. My master's man.   Strato, where is thy master?

Str. Free from the bondage you are in, Messala,
  The conquerors can but make a fire of him;
  For Brutus only overcame himself,
  And no man else hath honour by his death.

Lucil. So Brutus should be found.   I thank thee, Brutus,
  That thou hast prov'd Lucilius' saying true.

Oct. All that serv'd Brutus, I will entertain them.   60
  Fellow, wilt thou bestow thy time with me?

Str. Ay, if Messala will prefer me to you.

Oct. Do so, good Messala.

Mes. How died my master, Strato?

Str. I held the sword, and he did run on it.

Mes. Octavius, then take him to follow thee,
  That did the latest service to my master.

Ant. This was the noblest Roman of them all:
  All the conspirators, save only he,
  Did that they did in envy of great Cæsar: 70
  He, only in a general honest thought,
  And common good to all, made one of them.
  His life was gentle, and the elements

So mix'd in him, that Nature might stand up,
And say to all the world, ' This was a man ! '

Oct. According to his virtue, let us use him
With all respect, and rites of burial.
Within my tent his bones to-night shall lie,
Most like a soldier order'd honourably.
So call the field to rest, and let 's away,   80
To part the glories of this happy day.   *Exeunt*

Notes

I. i. 24. *withal I am*; so F. Most modern editors follow Steevens in over-emphasising the pun by reading *matters, but with awl. I am* . . .

I. ii. 266. *man of any occupation*; usually explained as ' man of any trade' (a common sense of *occupation*). But that seems pointless, and the phrase surely means, ' If I had been a man with any gift for seizing the occasion.'

I. iii. 65. *old men, fools, and children calculate*; so F. The passage is obscure—the chief difficulty being *calculate*—but none of the suggested emendations, such as *old men fool and children calculate*, seem to improve matters. The real trouble is that we do not want a verb till we arrive at *change* in the next line, that therefore *calculate* should be an adjective, and that there is no satisfactory sense for it.

II. i. 83. *put*; F reads *path*; if we retain this we are left with a verb of which the rarity is a much less serious difficulty than its lack of suitability, and an awkward absolute construction *thy native semblance on*. The natural run of the line seems to demand an active verb. The usual emendation is *put'st*, which is graphically harder than *put*, with the *th* following.

II. i. 114. *face*; so F, and heroic attempts have been made to defend it; but no explanation really makes the phrase adequately parallel to the two in the next line. But even the obvious *fate* seems to be of too general application to make it wholly acceptable.

II. i. 285. *suburbs*; the phrase begins, as it were, by meaning no more than its face value, *i.e.* ' in the outskirts of your affection.' But the suburbs were traditionally the haunts of prostitutes, and this *double entendre* perhaps led up to, and is certainly emphasised by, l. 287.

II. ii. 46. *We are two lions*; F *We heare two*; this, the usual, emendation is far from satisfactory, but gives the obvious sense.

II. ii. 89. *tinctures . . .*; of these four words *cognizance* has normally a heraldic significance; *stains and relics* seem to refer rather to the habit of securing mementos of martyrs; *tinctures* is normally heraldic, but might be merely an equivalent for *stains*. It looks as though there was some confusion of thought, since on Decius' *favourable* interpretation of the dream the heraldic significance is much more appropriate to the *living* Cæsar, dispensing distinctions to ' great men,' whereas the ' martyr' significance is much more appropriate to what actually occurred.

II. iv. 22. *ninth hour*; this should mean 3 p.m.; but since Cæsar at the end of II. ii. invites his friends in to drink wine shortly after 8 a.m. before going 'straightway' to the Capitol, it must surely mean 9 a.m.

III. i. 39. *law*; Johnson's emendation of F *lane*, which, unless there is some topical allusion which we have lost, seems meaningless. M. Macmillan suggests *lune*, i.e. 'caprice,' cp. *Winter's Tale*, I. ii. 170.

III. i. 47. *Cæsar doth not wrong . . .*; Ben Jonson made two adversely critical comments on this line, one in the *Discoveries* and one in *Staple of News*. Both times the reading is given as *Cæsar did never wrong but with just cause*, and as Jonson's criticism is that the line is absurd (which as it stands in F it is not) we may assume that that is what Shakespeare originally wrote. There is no way of determining whether it was Shakespeare or his editors who restored logic by a sacrifice of vigour and metre. The line in the original form seems to me so completely Shakespearean in its

116

anacoluthic expressiveness, and also so typical of the Shakespearean Cæsar, that I believe it should be restored to the text.

III. i. 171. *And pity . . .*; F punctuates the passage thus:

> *And pitty to the generall wrong of Rome,*
> *As fire drives out fire, so pitty, pitty*
> *Hath done this deed on Cæsar.*

If we like the emphatic repetition of *pitty* we can take *As fire drives out fire* as the parenthesis, with the second part of the parallel suppressed, and the repeated *pitty* as the subject of *hath done*. But it should be pointed out that the comma between the two *pitty*'s is of no significance either way, since it would be quite normal if the phrase meant 'so pity drives out pity.'

III. i. 175. *Our arms in strength of malice*; so F, and it is possible to defend the reading by taking it to mean that 'our arms are as little strong in malice as brothers' would be,' but the phrase is awkward. Various emendations have been proposed, *no strength*, *unstring their*, *in strength of amity*, and soon, without end. The best 'run' of the phrase is secured by the change to a verb, such as *unstring*.

III. i. 239-43. This passage is an excellent example of the dangers attendant on a cavalier treatment of the original punctuation. The text here given is that of F, and its sense is quite clear. Brutus is going to speak first, and is going to explain that Antony speaks only by permission. He then goes on to put an additional argument to Cassius for allowing Antony to speak, namely, that for the people to see that the conspirators are contented that Cæsar shall have all true rites will do them more good than harm. The punctuation of modern editions makes Brutus say that *in his speech* he will announce

that they are so contented (which in fact he does not do) and end
with an awkwardly abrupt single line; thus:

> *When Antony shall speak, I will protest*
> *He speaks by leave and by permission,*
> *And that we are contented Cæsar shall*
> *Have all true rites and lawful ceremonies.*
> *It shall advantage more than do us wrong.*

III. ii. 13-35. The Folio punctuation is retained throughout this
speech, as a perfect example of careful Elizabethan punctuation.

IV. i. 37. *objects, arts*; Theobald's emendation, *abject orts* (or as
modified by Staunton for the better, *abjects, orts*) is as brilliant as all
Theobald's best; but perhaps more brilliant than sound. Antony's
point is not that Lepidus is *mean*-spirited, so that he 'feeds on'
trifles which others reject, but that he is *barren*-spirited, *i.e.* wholly
unoriginative, so that he feeds on 'objects' (see N.E.D. 'a
gazing-stock') or second-hand imitations of them (*i.e.* he is a typical
'rubber-neck').

IV. ii. 50-52. *Lucilius . . . Lucius*; so F. Craik is somewhat assertively sure that the names should be transposed: "It
is strange that no one should have been struck with the absurdity
of such an association as Lucius and Titinius for the guarding of
the door—an officer of rank and a servant boy—the boy too
being named first. Nothing can be clearer than that Lucilius in
the first line is a misprint for Lucius, and Lucius in the third a misprint for Lucilius." Perhaps neither the absurdity of the text nor
the clearness of the misprints is as great as Craik believes. In the
first place the association of Brutus' personal servant, whom he
may want to summon (as he does), with Titinius, the official military

'guard,' is hardly absurd: and, in any case, one cannot have it both ways with Lucius—if he is so humble in rank that his association with Titinius is absurd, then one may say that Brutus is more likely to send an officer of rank than his batman with his orders to his legion-commanders. (It is through Lucilius, with Titinius, that he sends his orders in iii. 138, and if there, why not here?) No doubt a confusion between Lucius and Lucilius is easy enough, but I can see no convincing reason for tinkering with the text.

IV. iii. (S.D.). The scene-break of modern editions is here worse than needless. The F stage-direction, after *guard our door*, is *Exeunt. Manet Brutus, and Cassius*. Clearly, they draw the curtains of the back-stage, which represents Brutus' tent, and enter it.

IV. iii. 155. *swallowed fire*; according to the tradition given by Plutarch, this was literally true: she took burning coals into her mouth, and closed her lips till she choked to death.

IV. iii. 183. *Nothing, Messala*; unless we are to suppose that Brutus is making a dishonest parade of his stoicism to impress Messala, we have in this scene clear signs of revision, since the announcement of Portia's death by Messala needs to precede Brutus' announcement of it to Cassius, or, preferably, to disappear altogether. It will be noticed that 142-56 could be omitted with no awkwardness (except that Lucius must be quick with the wine); *i.e.* that these lines may easily be a later, and highly effective, addition.

V. ii. 5. *And*; it is tempting to read *One* (the confusion of minuscule *a* with *o* followed by a minim, and *e:d* makes it not impossible).

Glossary

MANY words and phrases in Shakespeare require glossing, not because they are in themselves unfamiliar, but for the opposite reason, that Shakespeare uses in their Elizabethan and unfamiliar sense a large number of words which seem so familiar that there is no incentive to look for them in the glossary. It is hoped that a glossary arranged as below will make it easy to see at a glance what words and phrases in any particular scene require elucidation. A number of phrases are glossed by what seems to be, in their context, the modern equivalent rather than by lexicographical glosses on the words which compose them.

Act First

SCENE I

line

3 MECHANICAL, artisans
12 DIRECTLY, straightforwardly
15 NAUGHTY, worthless
17 OUT, cross
26 NEATS-LEATHER, ox-hide

line

47 REPLICATION, re-echoing
66 CEREMONIES, adornments
70 TROPHIES, emblems
71 VULGAR, common people
74 PITCH, height

SCENE II

27 GAMESOME, in the mood for amusement
35 BEAR A HAND, *met. from riding a horse*
40 PASSIONS OF SOME DIFFERENCE, conflicting emotions
42 GIVE SOME SOIL TO MY BE-HAVIOURS, spoil my manners

59 OF THE BEST RESPECT, the most respected
71 JEALOUS ON, suspicious of
72 DID USE, was accustomed to
73 STALE, make common
76 SCANDAL, slander
86 IN, before
87 INDIFFERENTLY, impartially

GLOSSARY

Act I Sc. ii—*continued*

line
91 FAVOUR, appearance
119 HEARTS OF CONTROVERSY, contending spirits
136 COLOSSUS, the gigantic statue bestriding the harbour at Rhodes
156 ROOM, *pun on 'Rome' then pronounced 'room'*

line
163 I AM NOTHING JEALOUS, I have no doubt
217 SAD (*not quite the ordinary meaning 'sober,' 'solemn'*), put out, disgruntled
244 CHOPP'D, chapped
254 FALLING-SICKNESS, epilepsy
266 SAD, *see gloss on line* 217
314 BEAR ME HARD, dislike me

SCENE III

12 SAUCY, presumptuous
18 SENSIBLE OF, sensitive to
21 GLAZ'D, stared
22 DRAWN UPON, huddled into
32 CLIMATE, region
48 UNBRACED, with doublet unfastened
49 THUNDER-STONE, thunder-bolt
50 CROSS, forked
77 PERSONAL ACTION, physical capacity

84 SUFFERANCE, patience
108 TRASH, rubbish (*esp.* twigs)
109 OFFAL, rubbish (*esp.* chips of wood)
115 DANGERS ARE TO ME INDIFFERENT, I am indifferent to dangers
117 FLEERING, sneering
118 FACTIOUS, active
128 ELEMENT, sky
129 FAVOUR, appearance

Act Second

SCENE I

26 DEGREES, steps
29 WILL BEAR NO COLOUR FOR THE THING HE IS, will carry no conviction in view of what he actually is

33 HIS, its
66 MORTAL INSTRUMENTS, 'bodily machine'
76 MARK OF FAVOUR, physical peculiarity

Act II Sc. i—*continued*

line		line	
104	FRET, bar	206	TOILS, snares
115	SUFFERANCE, suffering	210	HUMOUR, mood
119	LOTTERY, at his allotted time	250	HUMOUR, moodiness
126	PALTER, break faith	261	PHYSICAL, healthy
129	CAUTELOUS, crafty	262	UNBRAC'D, *see gloss on* I. iii. 58
134	INSUPPRESSIVE, insuppressible		HUMOURS, mists
150	BREAK WITH, open our design to	266	RHEUMY, causing cold
178	ENVIOUS, liable to censure	307	ENGAGEMENTS, undertakings
197	CEREMONIES, omens	308	ALL THE CHARACTERY OF, all that
204	TREES, *i.e. charging and getting*		is written on
	stuck	315	WEAR A KERCHIEF, be ill
205	GLASSES, mirrors		

SCENE II

13	STOOD ON CEREMONIES, paid attention to omens	104	LIABLE, subservient

Act Third

SCENE I

line		line	
29	ADDRESS'D, ready	205	BAY'D, brought to bay
35	PREVENT, stop	207	SIGN'D IN THY SPOIL, stained
39	FOND, foolish		with thy blood
67	APPREHENSIVE, capable of apprehending		LETHE, death
69	RANK, course	217	PRICK'D, marked down
75	BOOTLESS, unavailingly	272	ATE, goddess of destruction
101	STAND UPON, trouble about	274	CRY 'HAVOC,' give signal for
106	BASIS, *sc.* of the statue		general slaughter and pillage
143	PRESENTLY, at once	283	BIG, full
		295	ISSUE, outcome of action

SCENE II

line	line
4 PART THE NUMBERS, divide the crowd	40 EXTENUATED, minimised
16 CENSURE, judge	41 ENFORC'D, emphasised
32 RUDE, uncouth	245 DRACHMA, a Greek silver coin (*roughly a shilling*)
38 THE QUESTION OF HIS DEATH, IS ENROLL'D IN THE CAPITOL, the whole debate about his death is recorded in the archives	253 PLEASURES, pleasure-grounds
	272 ARE RID, have ridden

SCENE III

2 UNLUCKILY CHARGE MY FANTASY, ominously weigh on my mind

Act Fourth

SCENE I

1 PRICK'D, marked	14 THE THREE-FOLD WORLD DIVIDED, *sc.* among the triumvirs
9 CUT OFF SOME CHARGE, cut down expense	48 STAKE, *i.e.* to which the bear was tied

SCENE II

23 HOLLOW, empty	46 ENLARGE, give vent
HOT AT HAND, spirited at the start	

SCENE III

2 NOTED, put the mark against	47 SPLEEN, *as the seat of anger*
8 NICE, petty	75 INDIRECTION, underhand means
44 BUDGE, give way	95 BRAV'D, defied

Act IV Sc. iii—*continued*

line

101 PLUTUS, the god of the underworld and so of precious metals
119 HUMOUR, temper
132 CYNIC, surly fellow
135 KNOW, recognise
    HUMOUR, pose
    TIME, fit time

line

136 JIGGING, rhyming
137 COMPANION, fellow
154 DISTRACT, out of her mind
164 CALL IN QUESTION, review
227 NIGGARD, 'give a small payment on account'
267 MACE, staff of office
290 FALSE, out of tune

Act Fifth

SCENE I

10 BRAVERY, display
    FACE, show
19 EXIGENT, crisis
33 POSTURE, quality

76 HELD STRONG, adhered firmly to
105 PREVENT, anticipate
106 TIME, appointed end

SCENE II

1 BILLS, orders

SCENE III

101 MOE, more (*Eliz. plural*)

105 FUNERALS, 'funerailles'

SCENE V

46 SMATCH, smattering
62 PREFER, recommend

81 PART, share